Quality Classroom Practices
for Professors

1994
Cornesky & Associates Inc.
489 Oakland Park Blvd.
Port Orange, FL 32127
Phone: 800-388-8682
Fax 904-756-6755

CORNESKY & ASSOCIATES, Inc., 1994

First Printing August 1994

Library of Congress Cataloging-in-Publication Data

ISBN 1-881807-06-1

CONTENTS

Table of Contents

LIST OF ILLUSTRATIONS

About the author . . .

Robert Cornesky is the author and/or co-author of numerous books and articles on Total Quality Management, including *Using Deming to Improve Quality in Colleges and Universities, Implementing Total Quality Management in Higher Education, The Quality Teacher: Implementing Total Quality Management in the Classroom, Quality Fusion: Turning Total Quality Management in Classroom Practice,* and *The Quality Professor: Implementing TQM in the Classroom.* Bob has over 25 years experience in higher education across the nation. He began his academic career first as an Instructor then to an Assistant Professor of Biological Sciences at Carnegie Institute of Technology (which later became Carnegie Mellon University). After moving to California State College at Bakersfield, Bob became an Associate Professor then later a full Professor of Biology. He entered academic administration at California State College, Bakersfield when he became Chairman of the Department of Health Sciences. Then he moved to an upper division and graduate institution, Governors State University in Illinois, where he became the Director of the School of Health Sciences and an University Professor. Later he became a Professor and Dean of a School of Allied Health at Texas Tech University Health Sciences Center. Finally Bob served as the Dean of a School of Science, Management & Technologies at Edinboro University of Pennsylvania, a comprehensive state university. Presently, Bob is the Editor of the *TQM in Higher Education* Newsletter and an educational consultant specializing in total quality management. His address is 489 Oakland Park Blvd., Port Orange, Florida 32127; phone (800) 388-8682; Fax (904) 756-6755.

I must close with a warning. Once people have learned to walk, they will not return to crawling. Once students have tasted the joy of learning in an educational institution which runs according to quality management principles, they will not accept something inferior.

Myron Tribus

MISSION

To facilitate effective instructor—student partnerships through the study of total quality management (TQM) principles and to demonstrate to the instructors how they can make a difference in their classrooms, institutions, and communities.

Robert A. Cornesky

Introduction

In 1987, while Dean of the School of Science, Management & Technologies (SM&T) at Edinboro University of Pennsylvania (EUP), I worked with my seven department chairs and several faculty in an attempt to implement total quality management (TQM) philosophies and practices. One of the main reasons for doing this was to break down the barriers between 120 faculty members and myself.

The working relations between the faculty and management at EUP were, at best, poor. The union's executive committee that represented the faculty always seemed to be at odds with the president and the provost. Both sides demonstrated adequate management protocol, but neither really displayed true leadership. To circumvent this "war" within SM&T, the department chairs (who were also unionized faculty) and I began our quality journey with the faculty by concentrating on the processes within the systems in which we were forced to work. As a result of these efforts, we published a book *Using Deming to Improve Quality in Colleges and Universities* (Madison, WI: Magna Publications, Inc., 1990). This was the first book to demonstrate that TQM was applicable to institutions of higher education, and in fact, it became the "quality manual" for SM&T!

There were some exciting things that began to happen in the School of SM&T as the faculty, chairs, staff, and I began to "walk-the-talk" of TQM, rather than "stumble-the-mumble." Productivity and morale of both faculty and staff increased. Many great ideas were constantly introduced and acted upon. In addition, student retention increased significantly, especially in the sciences and math.

As a result of some of the perceived successes within SM&T, Sam McCool, my assistant, Larry Byrnes, the Dean of the School of Education, and Bob Weber, the Dean of the School of Liberal Arts joined me in writing the next book, *Implementing Total Quality Management in Higher Education* (Madison, WI: Magna Publications, Inc., 1991). This publication was the first book to include a Malcolm Baldrige-Type assessment tool for educational institutions.

As a result of these two books, I was asked to consult with a number of colleges and universities to start them on their TQM journey. It became apparent, however, that the tools and techniques of total quality improvement were not adequately explained for either managers or faculty of educational institutions. So Sam McCool and I wrote another book: *Total Quality Improvement Guide for Institutions of Higher Education* (Madison, WI: Magna Publications, Inc., 1992).

For the most part, the books mentioned above really addressed the administrative side of the academy. The next logical step was the real

Every job is a self-portrait of the person who did it. Autograph your work with excellence.

challenge: Implementing TQM into classroom practice. Rising to the challenge was Margaret Byrnes, the wife of Larry Byrnes.

I introduced Margaret to the concepts of TQM and how they could be applied to running not only manufacturing organizations, but service organizations, health care organizations, and educational institutions as well. Margaret had the ability to take these complicated concepts and to apply them to the K-12 classroom setting. I have always said that TQM will fail in our educational system **unless we apply it from the boardrooms to the classrooms** in all of our educational institutions, and that includes K-20. So in 1992 Margaret Byrnes came and visited me in Florida where we wrote *The Quality Teacher: Implementing Total Quality Management in the Classroom* (Port Orange, FL : Cornesky & Associates, Inc., 1992). The book was directed for K-12 teachers and was based on the Malcolm Baldrige Quality Criteria and had examples of the commonly used total quality improvement tools and techniques.

We believed one of the reasons the TQM approach would work is that it encourages teamwork and collaboration. We said that classroom TQM is **a procedure wherein everyone in the class knows the objectives of the class and adopts a quality philosophy to continuously improve the work done to meet the objectives.** We stated that the general principles and tools of TQM encourage everyone in the classroom to identify inadequate processes and systems and recommend improvements, and that **TQM is not a rigid set of rules and regulations but processes and procedures for improving performance.**

The Quality Teacher text clarified TQM processes and procedures and demonstrated how they can be used in the classroom. The book, an introductory guide to teachers interested in implementing TQM in their classroom, summarizes the TQM approaches of the late W. Edwards Deming and Philip Crosby; introduces a Quality Index Self-Assessment tool that is based on the points of the Malcolm Baldrige National Quality Award Criteria; discusses specific ways to integrate each of the Malcolm Baldrige National Quality Award Criteria into the classroom; and explains the Total Quality Improvement tools. The book became a best seller!

However, too many teachers wanted more of prescriptive approach than was provided by *The Quality Teacher*. I suggested to Margaret that we satisfy this demand by taking a total quality management-based procedure and weaving it through a modified Foxfire educational approach by Eliot Wigginton (1985). The Foxfire educational approach consists of 11 core practices from a 25 year old approach started in Appalachia; however, we modified it and then fused it with the TQM principles of Deming and other quality experts to produce *Quality Fusion.* (Port Orange, FL : Cornesky & Associates, Inc., 1994).

Teaching in the college classroom is different from teaching in the K-12 setting. To meet the growing demands of college professors, I was encouraged by Ted Marchese of the AAHE to write a book for use in the college classroom. The result was a lengthy manuscript that was marvelously edited to 209 pages by Jennifer Lind, Bob Magnan, Linda Babler, Peter Voigt, and Doris Green of Magna Publications, Inc. The book is called *The Quality Professor: Implementing TQM in the (college) Classroom* (Madison, WI : Magna Publications, Inc., 1993). *The Quality Professor* book should be read prior to this book as it describes the approaches and principles to classroom TQM and the total quality improvement tools and techniques used in the classroom. In addition, it has a self-assessment tool based on the Malcolm Baldrige Quality Criteria that can help you identify where you are before you start your quality journey.

However, many of the younger professors, whose role model for teaching was the older professor who mostly lectured, wanted more of a prescriptive procedure than I described in *The Quality Professor*. Therefore, to get these professors started on their quality journey in teaching, I took the core in *Quality Fusion* and incorporated them in this book that I have named *Quality Classroom Practices for Professors*.

Quality Classroom Practices for Professors uses an educational approach that actively involves the students ("workers") in the learning system as they meet customer expectations, including parent, employer, and the instructor down the line. This book is developed for professors who are partially trained and knowledgeable about TQM principles and approaches and who want to apply the theory of TQM to their classrooms. For these professors, I offer a technique that will maximize professor and student successes while the professor expands and develops more fully his/her experiences into her/his personal quality approach.

The processes within the *Quality Classroom Practices for Professors* approach are meant to be modified to meet the needs of teaching and learning; however, modifications are not advised until you understand totally the principles and approaches of TQM. If you do understand the concepts of TQM, then I suggest that you use a holistic approach to the following steps rather than a linear approach. The *Quality Classroom Practices for Professors* approach, the core of my initial training program, involves eleven steps. The steps are listed below. This book will devote a chapter to each point as I attempt to guide you on your quality journey.

Quality is never an accident; it is always the result of high intention, sincere effort, intelligent direction and skillful execution; it represents the wise choice of many alternatives.
Willa A. Foster

1. The mission, goals, and academic integrity of the class must be absolutely clear.

Professors should have a clearly stated mission statement for each of their courses. The customers, including the students, should have considerable

The most effective way I know to begin with the end in mind is to develop a personal mission statement ...

Stephen Covey

input for defining not only the goals, but also how the goals will be met. The students should be expected to master the stated terminal competencies of the course. They should also recognize the value in the content area being taught and its connections to other disciplines.

2. The professor must demonstrate leadership.

The professor's role is that of a coach, collaborator, and team leader, rather than boss. S/he monitors the academic and social growth of every student, leading each into new areas of understanding and competence.

3. Most work must be pertinent and flow from the students.

Much of the work professors and students do can best be done as teams and must flow from student desire and student concerns. From the beginning the work should be infused with student choice, design, revision, execution, reflection and evaluation. Professors should take on some of the responsibility for assessing and ministering to the developmental needs of the students.

When a student asks, "Here's a situation that just came up. I don't know what to do about it. What should I do?" the professor turns the question back to the class to wrestle with and solve, rather than simply answering it. Students are trusted continually, and all are led to the point where they embrace responsibility.

4. Course content is connected to the campus community and the real world.

If you connect the content of your course to the campus community and the real world, students will be more willing to engage in meaningful discussions and projects. For example, in an economics course the students may find that, at some future time, the cost of treating people for AIDS may not be feasible if the epidemic continues to spread and/or if new drugs are not found to treat the disease. Likewise, when students are excited about the relevancy of the course competencies, they will meet after class and discuss environmental issues, prejudice, drugs, rape, alcohol, etc. They actually will bring these issues "home" to the campus community and their residence.

5. The student is not only treated as a "worker," but also as a team member of the "research and development" department.

If the professor considers himself to be the "manager" of the classroom, the student can be considered as the "worker" responsible for a large part of the product (learning). This concept means that the work is characterized by action wherein the students actively processes information as they complete the terminal competencies of the course.

However, your course should be designed so that after acquiring new information, students should be able to apply it to new course content in new ways. The atmosphere of constantly applying "research and development" techniques (the scientific method, critical thinking, logic, etc.) to routine class meetings should be firmly established.

When classes are run in such a manner, students will make mistakes. It should be clear to every student that mistakes will always occur when new things are tried—that's just part of "research and development."

6. Peer teaching, small group work, and team work are emphasized.

A constant feature in *Quality Classroom Practices for Professors* is its emphasis on peer teaching, small group work, and team work. Every student should be involved in helping each other master the expected terminal competencies.

7. Students should have aesthetic experiences.

Professors usually have many artistic examples that can be applied to not only their course, but to life in general. They should recognize the worth of aesthetic experiences and resist teaching practices that deprive students of the chance to use their imaginations. From these experiences students develop their capacities to appreciate, to refine, to express, to enjoy and to break out of restrictive, unproductive modes of thought.

8. Classroom processes should include reflection.

The professor should mandate that five minutes of each class be set aside for reflection. This is an essential activity if the students and professor want to consider how the present teaching/learning system is to be improved. Since this is the activity that professors and students are least accustomed to doing, the professors will have to dedicate themselves to this undertaking.

9. The teaching/learning system should undergo constant evaluation.

Obviously, the professor will have to evaluate the work produced by each student. There are a number of ways in which this is done. I believe that the mastery of most terminal competencies should be evaluated by a variety of testing strategies. Nevertheless, the professor should ask: "In what ways will you prove to me at the end of this class that you have mastered the objectives we have designed?"

Appraisal is an expensive way of getting quality. What has to happen is prevention. The error that does not exist cannot be missed.
Philip Crosby

Students should be trained to develop portfolios and to monitor their own progress then devise their own improvement plans. Students should understand that the **success** of each student is the **job** of every other student since working together will help advance society (and reduce prejudice).

If the student works closely with a professor in developing his/her portfolio, the professor will have a valuable resource to evaluate the learning experience of the student. In addition, the portfolio, if kept on file, will provide the professor with information that is often required for letters of recommendation.

10. New activities should constantly evolve from the old.

As the course progresses, newly acquired competencies should evolve gracefully out of the previous ones.

The students should understand that their quest for quality work is never ending and that the "product" of one class is nothing more than the "raw" material for another advanced "product."

The questions at the end of each class period, as well as at the end of each course, should be: "Now what? What do we know that we didn't know when we started out together? How can we use these skills and this information in some new, more complex and interesting ways? What's next?"

11. There must be an audience beyond the professor.

The students should be recognized for their achievement by audiences other than the professor.

There are many ways to recognize students. One of my personal favorites is by having an oral report of a research project by each team. I preferred to set aside an evening meeting time for these reports and I invited community groups, business leaders, university administrators, and other faculty to these meetings.

If you can't measure it, you cannot manage it or improve it.

I strongly suggest that before you begin implementing the aforementioned points in your teaching practices you may wish to consider doing a **Quality Index Rating Profile** of your classroom processes and systems as described in Chapter Nine of *The Quality Professor: Implementing TQM in the Classroom* (Madison, WI: Magna Publications, 1993). This will give you a baseline from which to begin your continuous quality improvement (CQI) journey. Since CQI results are sometimes incremental, I suggest that you redo the assessment and compare the results with your student evaluations after each semester of applying and then improving upon your classroom quality efforts. I think you'll really be surprised with the results. (Magna Publications, Inc., can be contacted at 2718 Dryden Drive, Madison, WI 53704-3086; PH; 608-246-3580.)

Chapter One: The mission, goals, and academic integrity of the class must be absolutely clear.

ESTABLISH A CLASSROOM MISSION

The first three habits of highly effective people according to the best selling book by Stephen R. Covey (*The 7 Habits of Highly Effective People.* NY: Simon & Schuster, 1989) are:

1. **Be Proactive,**
2. **Begin with the End in Mind,** and
3. **Put first things first.**

Applied to the classroom, being proactive enables you to create actions in response to particular circumstances.

Beginning with the end in mind means that you should have not only a personal mission statement, but also a classroom mission statement upon which the classroom goals are based. Your classroom mission statement should reflect a shared vision within your institution and a reference point by which your students (and you) will conduct themselves.

Putting first things first, according to Covey (p. 147) is *the day-in, day-out, moment-by-moment doing it.*

Covey's first three habits are closely aligned with Deming's (1982) first point: **Create a constancy of purpose toward improvement of product and service.**

When you begin your continuous quality improvement (CQI) journey towards a quality classroom (Be Proactive), you should have a firmly established view of your course mission (Begin with the End in Mind), and you should have adopted short- and long-range plans to implement your mission statement and to improve upon it through years of "research and development" (Put First Things First).

Without having a constancy of purpose, *i.e.,* a clearly defined mission statement and a plan to implement it, you will be driven by reactions to immediate concerns and you will have the tendency to move in a random fashion in order to satisfy the immediate needs of an "instant gratification" society.

Unless you and your students have a clear view at a very fundamental level of what the basic goals and academic integrity of your class are, both you and your students will have no map to guide your personal development.

The need for course mission statements might seem obvious, but seldom do I see them in classrooms around the country.

Developing a mission is not as easy as it may seem. It essentially defines the purpose of one's work. Professors without a clear mission statement have little or no idea of their goals in either the short term, or the long term. If your

There are more things in heaven and earth, Horatio, Than are dreamt of in your philosophy.
Shakespeare

mission is **to teach world geography,** you may feel that you are being successful in spite of the fact that 50 percent of your students are not learning. If no one learns, you can't claim to have taught. Remember, colleges don't exist for professors to teach, but for students to learn. Therefore, the professor has not viewed **learning** as the primary purpose if this is his/her classroom mission statement.

Professors must focus away from teaching and towards learning. Quality professors lead students and facilitate the learning process. The interaction between professor and learner must be shifted so more responsibility for learning is placed on the student, and more facilitating is done by the professor.

Professors should take an initial leadership role in creating the learning environment. As the semester progresses, however, professors should increase gradually the leadership responsibilities of **all** students. Students should be partners in co-creating the learning experiences and in establishing a learning environment where everyone can succeed. As the professor exerts less control, s/he should mentor students to become more active in their own learning.

Let's assume the professor has carefully reflected and determined his/her classroom mission to be:

To facilitate learning about the world so all students can understand how the regional, national, and international economies are related in order for the students to advance our society.

Now, this is a much better classroom (or course) mission statement since learning replaces teaching as the primary purpose. In addition, the reasons why the learning is important are stated.

A little learning is a dangerous thing;
Drink or taste not the Pierian spring.
　　　　　　　Pope

A teacher affects eternity; he can never tell where his influence stops.
　　　　　　Henry Adams

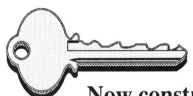

Now construct your own classroom mission statement.

My Classroom Mission Statement is:

Is your classroom mission statement aligned with the institutional mission?

Once you have carefully constructed your mission statement and reflected upon it, you should constantly ponder how it might be improved. You should reflect and record how you put "first things first," *i.e.*, the important and urgent activities you do to support your mission statement, and the relatively unimportant and not urgent things you do which impede your mission statement. What are your opportunities for improvement? Place your thoughts and observations into the following time management matrix.

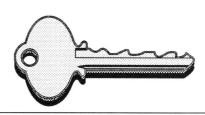

TIME MANAGEMENT MATRIX

	Urgent	Not Urgent
Important	**I** Activities: Improvement Opportunities	**II** Activities: Improvement Opportunities
Not Important	**III** Activities: Improvement Opportunities	**IV** Activities: Improvement Opportunities

Things I do to enhance my mission statement are:

Actions I will take to ensure that I continue to do these things:

Things I do to impede my mission statement are:

Actions I will take to overcome these things:

SELF-IMPROVEMENT PROGRAM

Covey states (p. 151) that **important** matters have to do with results. *If something is important, it contributes to your mission, your values, your high priority goals.* If you don't have a clear idea of your classroom mission statement and the results you would like to have your students achieve under your leadership, you will react to **urgent** matters, including the important and unimportant matters.

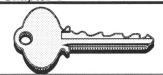

My self improvement program for this year will include:

My goals for this year are:

My goals for years two and three are:

Your improvement program should be designed to help you reduce the behaviors that impede progress towards the mission and increase the supporting behaviors.

Continuously attempt to reduce any behavior that doesn't help you move the students toward the mission. Just as you occasionally need help to align your progress towards your mission, so will the students. Be patient with yourself and with each student.

DEVELOP YOUR GOALS

Once you've developed your mission statement based upon your convictions, it is time to make tentative goals for your course. Set the goals high enough so they will represent a stretch for you and your students. Each year your goals should be based on continuous quality improvement from the previous year. Goals should be measurable.

ACADEMIC INTEGRITY

Once you have established a course mission and goals that are aligned with the department's (or program's) mission and goals, familiarize yourself with the terminal course competencies that are expected by your colleagues. After all, your course is part of a curriculum that was (or should have been) designed by a group of faculty who considered the needs and requirements of internal and external customers. In any event, you should have the freedom to add to the expected terminal competencies of your course and to determine how best your students can achieve and demonstrate the mastery of the competencies. I recommend that the terminal competencies of your course be displayed prominently in the classroom and in the class syllabus. The purpose of all this is to impress upon you and your students the importance of the terminal competencies, especially in terms of your mission and hopefully, the way work is assessed. It is far too easy to lose sight of the required terminal competencies. Quality professors view terminal competencies as minimal standards and never as ultimate goals.

Students should be informed regularly about what is expected of them during the semester. Competencies can be clearly stated and explained to students so they understand what is expected.

When students co-create their learning experiences by working with you to determine the way they will learn something, you will discover that the competencies can be reached in ways you have not thought of. This beautiful blend is the result of students' becoming very highly motivated. The professor's job becomes much easier since students become focused. Of course, there is never enough time for you to accomplish everything that you would like to accomplish during the semester. Just resign yourself to that fact, especially if the students want to do additional work on a project or take another direction in solving a problem.

With each learning experience, professor and students together determine which competencies will be achieved when the experience is finished. It may take some time for the professor to put all the additional competencies on a chart, but the time is well spent since students can thereafter keep track of their own progress.

While I recommend tracking competencies, I remind you that the focus of the classroom experiences must remain on processes and not the competencies. Through the co-creation of learning experiences, learning can become such a joy for students and instructors alike that you'll undoubtedly discover that achievement will soar far beyond your original expectations. I caution you not to dilute the process improvement techniques called for in continuous quality improvement. The whole idea behind co-creation of the learning experience is that students and professors together determine the way(s) competencies will be achieved. There are infinite ways to master the same competencies, so allow yourself and the students to have fun while determining what road to take. Remember, not everyone has to take the same road. Students learn best in different ways, and there may even be instances when you have six or more different ways to achieve the end.

By maintaining a clear constancy of purpose and by having a written mission statement and a set of measurable goals, you will be able to align all activities within the course towards success. In this way, using the continuous quality improvement model, you'll be able to work with students, colleagues, and others to build quality into every process within your course. By building quality into each process, the result will be a much higher level of achievement for all students, and you and they can experience the joy of learning!

Desire is the key to motivation, but it's the determination and commitment to an unrelenting pursuit of your goal—a commitment to excellence—that will enable you to attain the success you seek.
Mario Andretti

ΔΔΔΔΔΔΔΔΔ

The following is a checksheet tool to help the professor to implement the **Quality Fusion** technique into the classroom.

Step 1:   The mission, goals, and academic integrity of your course are absolutely clear.
√   Established a course mission statement.
√   Developed personal goals for the course.
√   Communicated mission and goals to the students.
√   Aligned course mission and goals with those of the department (program/major).

Chapter Two: The professor must demonstrate leadership.

The professor must have leadership, or a quality classroom is not obtainable. Leadership is the "Driver" of the quality system which results in customer satisfaction and success.

Leadership is what helps the professor in her/his role of coach, facilitator, collaborator and team leader, rather than boss. Leadership is the adeptness that directs the professor to monitor the academic and social evolution of every student, leading each into new areas of understanding and competence.

A professor has leadership qualities when s/he is able to:

> Bring students together into a cohesive group;
> Establish trust among the students;
> Convince everyone in the class to participate in establishing and/or refining the classroom mission;
> Clearly elaborate on the course competencies necessary for students in order for them to achieve their personally desired goals;
> Organize the class so that the students can think critically and resolve their conflicts as they continue to be supportive of all other members of the class;
> Create visibility for pride-in-workmanship;
> Involve the students in community projects;
> Constantly monitor and improve the teaching/learning system with input from stakeholders;
> Evaluate the results of each student; and
> Help students to realize that they must constantly renew and improve upon their previous efforts.

Habit 2 (Begin with the end in mind) is based on principles of personal leadership, which means that leadership is the first creation.

Stephen Covey

If you are to establish a quality driven classroom, you first have to know what it is. Without a clear and thorough understanding of a quality classroom, you may find it difficult to distinguish those practices and processes which are helpful from those which are harmful. Traditional teaching and classroom management styles do not afford you the opportunity for such an examination since they are based on the professor as manager rather than as leader.

Leadership for quality emphasizes empowerment of workers and focuses on customer satisfaction. Quality leaders also seek to inspire and lend support to suppliers, including high schools and previous professors, that they too may bring Total Quality to their courses. The combination of all these efforts demands that you assume a strong leadership role. While Total Quality seeks to strengthen the breadth of decision making and empowerment, it does not diminish the necessity for a depth of leadership from the chief executive (professor) that allows such a breadth to happen. In other words, while power is spread throughout the classroom, there remains the need to stay focused, set priorities, and maintain the highest standards.

What is a partner?

What actions encourage partnerships?

What actions discourage partnerships?

What actions do you take to encourage partnerships?

What actions do you take that discourage partnerships?

The bad news is that there are no quick approaches to quality leadership. Your leadership role is an evolutionary process that becomes more refined as the workers (students), suppliers (previous professors and high school teachers) and customers (students, subsequent professors, graduate schools, employers, and parents) provide valuable, indeed irreplaceable, feedback that allows you to grow while your classrooms advance towards quality. Remember, within the classroom, the professor assumes the role of top leadership, and, therefore, s/he must find ways to empower the students to become **partners** in the improvement process.

DRIVER OF THE SYSTEM
Leadership is the first category of the Malcolm Baldrige Quality Award criteria. It is also known as the "driver" of the total quality system, for without it, all else fails. It may also be the most difficult and diffuse to decipher because it seems to imply several things. One is that the leader must be strong. That might appear to be in direct contrast to the entire concept of empowering workers. However, Deming, Crosby, Juran and other Quality experts all agree on the importance of leadership for quality. One cannot ignore its significance. This means that as a quality professor, you will want to take time to give shape and distinction to your own definition of quality. Not only must you understand what quality is; you will have to be able to articulate it in words that students and colleagues can understand.

For example, let's assume that your department's mission statement is:

To prepare students with the knowledge, skills, and abilities necessary to become responsible and productive citizens in a global community.

Professors within this department should articulate their quality statements within the context of the department's statement. A math professor might have as her/his Quality Statement:

Quality work is defined by the ability to use logic, and to work individually and as teams to apply the mathematical concepts learned to real life situations.

I am assuming that you will take great care to prepare a quality statement, and then to articulate it to students and colleagues. Like your course mission statement, this can be a time-consuming process, but consider that it is the foundation for all that you will be doing within the classroom. Unless each of the participants understands what you are seeking, how can you expect them to take an interest in following your lead?

Avoid the temptation to "rush" into the course with the urge to cover the first chapter. It is exactly this rush to "get started" that has been at the root of teaching and learning failures for years.

Professors who have been involved in quality teaching have learned that students need to understand "why" before they become interested in "how." You simply must resist the urge to dive into the course content rather than allowing students to understand the straightforward answers to 'why' they are in this class and 'why' it is necessary for them to learn this content matter. In other words, students need to know how the information and skills gained in the class will be helpful and meaningful to their lives now and in the future. I will elaborate on this point in Chapter Four.

Quality professors recognize that this level of understanding flips the motivation factor from external to internal. Successful professors are experts at getting the students to recognize the basic worth and meaningfulness of any subject matter. This process may take a class period. Some professors have additional evening class meetings and/or office hours to discuss the "why-of-it." You should not consider this wasted time, but rather time to build the foundation upon which a quality class can stand. Proponents of quality teaching faithfully go through this process since in the end, students achieve more by the end of the semester than in a traditional setting.

WALK-THE-TALK

From the beginning, your leadership must reflect quality in every way. This is easier said than done, and once you begin your quality journey, you will be reminded daily how difficult, albeit exciting, it is. In short, there is no substitute for your displaying quality about every aspect of yourself or your actions both in and outside the classroom. You must "walk-the-talk."

Training students in quality begins before you ever enter the classroom. It begins with your commitment to becoming a quality professor, and it never ends. This is why it is so important to understand clearly what quality means to you. Anything less will surely leave you confused, frustrated, and disillusioned

Persistence is a very powerful habit. In fact, most successful people will rank this trait as one of their best. Maintain your quality vision, and at the same time be willing to alter the quality plan upward (never downward) as the organization (or your classroom) bumps against outside factors that require flexibility. Take the posture that each time the students test your commitment to quality, they are giving you a gift. That gift is a constant reaffirmation of your belief and conviction that Total Quality is the way to higher academic achievement.

In fact, leadership for quality will begin to permeate everything you are

---

Leadership Questions

What is your quality statement?

Does your quality statement relate directly to the mission statement of the class?

What have you done to communicate to your students **WHY** it is important for them to focus on quality results?

Do your students understand why they must be customer focused?

Do your students understand that in TQM theory that faulty processes and systems are the cause of most problems (and not a person)?

and do. When you adopt a customer focus, you'll find yourself looking at all your activities and commitments from a different point of view. As a customer to many, you'll find yourself asking: is this quality? Once that happens, then you can be sure that you are well on the way to adopting a leadership role rather than boss manager role.

With the customer focus and clearly defined ideas about what you want and expect, you will be able to align all classroom activities towards meeting your goal. If your goal is to have all students succeed at learning within your course, you must analyze all your course processes to determine if each process is in tune with your goal. If not, you have a critical determinant for a continuous improvement project.

The greatest thing in this world is not so much where we are, but in what direction we are moving.
O.W. Holmes

Either you have a quality classroom mission statement with a customer focus or you don't. You cannot change according to the time of year. For instance, two weeks before the end of the semester, you cannot dispense with your commitment to quality by thinking "I still have so much to cover." Your leadership commitment must be vital, strong, and totally focused at all times. Panicking at the end of the semester will not result in students' doing any more or any higher quality work.

The need for you as the leader to stay focused cannot be understated. Quality leaders demonstrate through actions what they are about. Having a written statement about quality and then saying things that drive in fear will confuse students. Not only is it important that your actions and statements be focused on quality, but also your personal appearance. People recognize those individuals who "walk their talk" rather than "stumble their mumble" to be the true leaders. Quality is not something that relates simply to what we do between 8 a.m. and 3 p.m. each day.

The need for professors to become quality role models has never been greater. It is an obligation of every professor to be a role model, but the Quality Professor sets continuously higher standards of excellence for himself/herself as well as for the students. Anything less will confuse students, making it more difficult for them to recognize quality and far less able to reach it.

The quality professor becomes more involved, rather than less involved. S/he makes time to speak about quality at every opportunity and points out quality wherever possible. One's presence at community meetings or functions, or faculty meetings sends strong messages to external customers and suppliers. In fact, these are viewed as important opportunities to keep the organization focused on quality.

A quality professor aligns every aspect of his/her work with the stated mission and goals. Along with this alignment comes a need to study and understand how students learn. Quality leadership is predicated on an understanding of Deming's system of profound knowledge. Profound knowledge holds the key to unlocking the secret of quality for professors and other leaders. Often a lack of understanding of **Profound Knowledge** (see below) is what is missing from leaders who attempt to build quality into their organizations only to have the organization fail.

PROFOUND KNOWLEDGE

Deming's system of profound knowledge appears simplistic but is very powerful. It states that in order to bring total quality management principles and processes into the organization (in our case, the classroom) one must have a thorough understanding of four concepts, namely, 1) an appreciation for a system, 2) statistical theory, 3) theory of knowledge, and 4) psychology. Let's examine these points briefly.

- **Appreciation for a system**
    > Education is a system with many sub-systems and processes within the subsystems.
    > The college or university is one large system.
    > Each level (school, department, program, course) represents a sub-system within the larger system.
    > Within each system numerous processes exist.
    > Deming and other quality experts agree that anywhere from 85-95% of all problems within an organization are due to faulty processes and systems. Management controls the system (*works on* the system), and therefore management must be responsible for taking the lead in changing it. Professors are managers of their course. Therefore, **understand that adopting a systems view means the focus is on improving processes —not results.**

You may be saying, "In my department I am evaluated on results and therefore must exert all my energy to covering the content and making certain the students learn." Don't confuse the issues of process improvement with student achievement. Inspection at the end (such as a test, the end of a semester) is simply too late to discover there was a process flaw that kept everyone from being successful. Quality must be built into every process before high quality results can follow. Quality classrooms focus more on process improvement while setting high quality expectations. Results do follow.

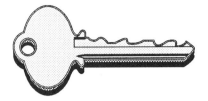

List the systems and/or the processes that are amenable to improvement in your course and the last time they were critically evaluated.

System (Processes)	Year Examined

What can you conclude from the above exercise? Where the systems that you identified actually reviewed and then improved, or was it business as usual?

• **Statistical theory**

Quality experts agree that the use of data is critical to know what action to take for process change. So often when data is not used, we tamper with processes not knowing the real problem(s).

In many respects, the failure to use statistics and meaningful data when working within a system that deals with people has led to a decline in the teaching/learning system.

Understanding statistical theory means that you must understand the concept of variation. You should learn what makes a system stable and unstable. You should know the "common causes" of variation (and how they are often mistaken as "special cause" variation), and the special causes of variation (and how they are often mistaken for common cause variation). You should understand how improper tampering with the system can create bigger and more difficult problems than if you had done nothing.

In higher education, a fairly common cause of poor learning is student boredom, yet it is often treated as a special cause. Common causes are those things that regularly recur due to normal statistical variation of the system. Student boredom is probably one of the biggest contributors to students' dropping out and/or not passing a course. Still, many believe that boredom is the student's problem and not a process problem. As a consequence, no action is taken to collect data, discover root causes, and implement an action plan for reducing boredom.

Special cause variation of why students might be missing your class might include:

- A high absentee rate due to a flu epidemic,
- The football team scheduled to play in a championship game, and
- The first snowfall of the year.

In order to fully understand the processes within the classroom, you will have to become familiar with simple statistical tools. They are not difficult to learn or understand. Even the various control charts can be made very simple through the use of computer software. Without the data, statistical tools, and a clear understanding of how to use them for process improvement, it is unsafe to assume that you can optimize any of the classroom processes.

I suggest that you refer to pages 144-170 in *The Quality Professor* (1993) to review the control charts and how they can be used to evaluate classroom systems. However, you might find the following example interesting. It was provided by Larry Sharp

ΔΔΔΔΔΔΔΔΔ

The Mean and Range Chart

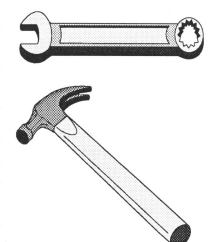

While administrative applications of most control charts are relatively easy to discern, especially the attributes control charts, classroom applications are more difficult to find. This is particularly true for the Mean and Range Chart, which depends on the availability of relatively homogeneous subgroups of equal size. Thoughtful reflection by a faculty member will however, reveal opportunities for use of the Mean and Range Chart.

For example, the instructor could track the teaching/learning process by charting the individual student performance on daily quizzes over time by using the Individual Mean and Range Chart as described in the April 1994 issue of *TQM in Higher Education* newsletter. Or, as we shall demonstrate, the performance of the entire class can be followed by using the Mean and Range Chart.

In this application, the subgroup is made up of all student scores for a quiz on a given day. Means and Ranges are determined over time. The instructor then examines the chart for evidence that overall class performance is improving. In this case s(he) is looking for evidence that the process is not stable. Evidence which would suggest this would be an upward trend in the mean class scores over time. Notice that in this case, a stable, in control process would signal that nothing special is happening to the class mean scores. If this were the case, class mean scores would randomly fluctuate around a relatively stable mean with no discernible trend. This would be evidence that neither the teaching strategy nor the students' attention to the material were producing any change in class mean.

Use of a class-wide Mean and Range Chart is particularly helpful if the instructor has adopted a Cooperative Learning Strategy whereby the class as a team is rewarded for improved performance and each student has a vital interest in other student's success. Shown below are the data from a small seminar section with five students and their scores on daily quizzes over 10 class periods.

Class #	Score 1	Score 2	Score 3	Score 4	Score 5	Mean	Range
1	6	5	7	6	4	5.6	3
2	5	7	6	6	7	6.4	2
3	7	6	6	7	7	6.6	1
4	6	7	8	7	6	6.8	2
5	7	7	6	7	7	6.8	1
6	7	8	6	8	8	7.4	2
7	7	8	8	7	8	7.6	1
8	8	9	7	8	7	7.8	2
9	8	7	9	9	8	8.2	2
10	8	9	9	9	8	8.6	1

PROCEDURE
1. Add the values for each row.
2. Find the average or mean for each row. (sum the values in each row and divide by 5)
3. Calculate the overall mean. Sum the row means and divide by 10 (5.6 + 6.4 + 6.6 +......+7.8 + 8.2 + 8.6) = 71.8/10 = 7.18 = $\overline{\overline{X}}$ which is the overall process mean.
4. Note the largest and smallest values in each row.
5. Determine the Range for each row by subtracting the smallest value from the largest value. This is the Range for each subgroup.
6. Find the Average Range ($\overline{R}$) by summing the 10 sub-group ranges and divide by 10 (3 + 2 + 1 + ...2 + 2 + 1) = 17. R bar = 17/10 = 1.7.

Calculate the Upper and Lower Control Limits for the Range Chart first.
This is typically done before the control limits for the Means Chart are calculated since the range chart analyzes variability *within* subgroups and it is this variability which is used to calculate the limits for the sub-group means chart. We expect variability *within* subgroups to be due only to inherent, common cause or random variability. We are interested in that variability which appears *across sub-groups* because it is that variability which tells us if the teaching/learning process is systematically changing.

1. Upper Control Limit for Ranges $UCL_R = D4 \times \overline{R}$. (D4 varies as a function of sample size; for a sub-groups of size 5 it is 2.114. This value comes from external sources and it is related to the standard deviation. Consult any statistical process control text for values of D4 for other sample sizes.)
2. $UCL_R = 2.114 \times 1.7$
3. $UCL_R = 3.6$
4. Draw a horizontal line across the Range Chart at the value of $\overline{R} = 1.7$ and label it $\overline{R}$
5. Draw a horizontal line across the Range Chart at the Value 3.6 and label it UCL_R.
6. Since the sample size is less than 6, draw a horizontal line across the Range Chart at the 0 value on the Y axis and label it LCL_R.
7. Plot each of the subgroup ranges on the range chart.

Interpret the Range Chart
Points outside the control limits would indicate the ranges are not in statistical control. In this application, this would mean that there are systematic differences between students. If this were the case, the instructor would consult the students whose ranges were beyond the UCL_R and try to generalize their learning strategies to the other students, especially those whose ranges might be closer to the LCL_R. In a similar fashion, the instructor would want to consult these latter students to determine the special cause of their lower performance.
Since the Range Chart reflects a process "in control", we can proceed to calculate the Means Chart Control Limits.

Calculate the Upper and Lower Control Limits for the Means Chart.
1. $UCL_X = \overline{\overline{X}} + (A2 \times R \text{ bar})$. (A2 varies as a function of sample size; for a sub-group of 5 (number of students), it is 0.577. This value comes from external sources and is related to the standard deviation. Consult any statistical process control text for other values of A2.

2. $UCL_X = 7.18 + (0.577 \times 1.7)$
3. $UCL_X = 7.18 + 0.98$
4. $UCL_X = 8.16$
5. Draw a horizontal line across the Means Chart at the value 8.16 on the Y axis and label it UCL_X.
   The Lower Control Limit for the Means Chart (LCL_X) is simply the process mean ($\overline{\overline{X}}$) minus the quantity (A2 x $\overline{R}$).
6. $LCL_X = 7.18 - (0.577 \times 1.7)$
7. $LCL_X = 7.18 - 0.98$.
8. $LCL_X = 6.2$

Notice how narrow are the control limits—6.2 to 8.16. This is so because the sub-group ranges have very little variation. We want this to be the case so that we maximize the likelihood of detecting a sub-group average exceeding these limits, thus indicating a change in process, hopefully on the high end.

9. Draw a horizontal line across the Means Chart at the value 6.2 on the Y axis and label it LCL_X.

10. Draw a horizontal line across the means chart at the value of the process mean ($\overline{\overline{X}}$) = 7.18 and label it $\overline{\overline{X}}$.

11. Plot each of the sub-group means on the Means Chart.

Interpret the Means Chart

While these data are hypothetical and specifically chosen to demonstrate the use of the Mean and Range Control Chart, the graph clearly shows the upward trend in mean scores over time. With addition of control limits, one can now assert with a high degree of confidence that the process demonstrates a non-chance increase in mean scores. That is, the mean values vary (systematically upward) due to factors other than chance and this variation can be attributed to the teaching/learning process and the continuous improvement strategies which the instructor has implemented. For example, if the instructor facilitated Cooperative Learning as a classroom strategy for this class section, but retained Competitive Learning in another section of the same class, s(he) would be able to compare the effects of the differing strategies by constructing a Mean and Range Chart for the second section.

It is important to reiterate that the purpose of the Mean Range Control Chart demonstrated here is to *detect a process not in statistical control ,* because the purpose is to demonstrate the influence of special causes of variation, for example, Cooperative Learning.

For more information contact: Lawrence F. Sharp, Ph.D., President and Principal Consultant, Six Sigma Enterprises, 2110 Vickers Drive Suite 100, Colorado Springs, Colorado 80918 1-719-598-8393. He specializes

in Quality Improvement Consulting for the Health Care and Education
communities.

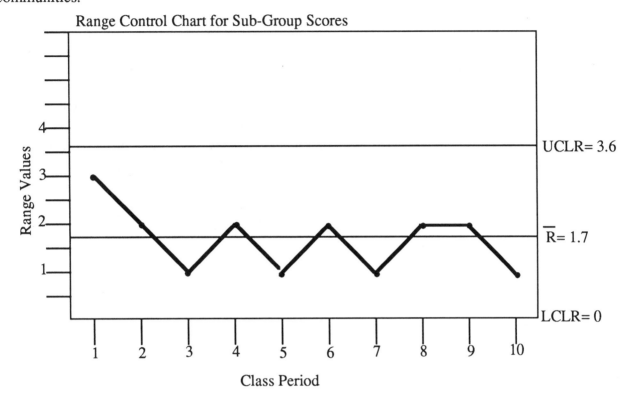

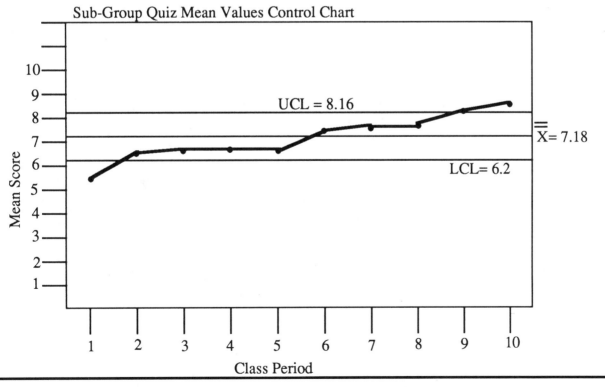

ΔΔΔΔΔΔΔΔ

- **Theory of Knowledge**

The experts use the following example to help clarify the theory of knowledge. If you took apart one model of each automobile produced and discovered the best transmission, the best ignition, the best engine, the best brakes, the best steering, etc. and analyzed what made them "the best," you could probably document it. But if you attempted to put each of these "best" parts into one automobile, you would soon discover that the car wouldn't run. The sum of the parts does not equal the whole. It is the way the parts interact with each other that creates a synergy that makes the car run.

Therefore, in thinking about education and the classroom specifically, we must remember that it is the way each of the processes interacts with the others that creates the quality classroom.

Professors who employ coercive tactics, even if it is with one or two students, alter the learning environment for everyone. Where fear is entrenched, people simply cannot do their best. Classrooms based on fear, ridicule, or humiliation are not places where students maintain a high interest or are eager to take educational risks to optimize their learning.

Theory of knowledge means that management understands the impact of change on the system. This places the burden on management (the professor) to engage in a Plan-Do-Check-Act (PDCA) cycle prior to making any change.

- **Psychology**

Professors must understand people and their needs. This means that we recognize five basic needs of people, namely, survival, love/respect, power, fun, and freedom. Every human behavior seeks to satisfy one or more of these needs. If you don't pay attention to these needs, then neither students nor colleagues will respond in ways that optimize the efficiency and effectiveness of your course and/or department.

Students' needs include power, fun, and freedom. Give yourself another reality check. How much power do the students in your classes have right now? Do they have any decision-making power? If so, who has it—everyone or only some of the students? How much fun do you and the students have in class? How do you define fun? What about freedom? Do students in your class(es) have any freedom or must everyone do the same thing at the same time in the same way?

No one takes pride in doing repetitive, dull, or watered down work. Students who are engaged in this kind of work view it as drudgery and may even begin to view your course as punishment. On the other hand, students who have the opportunity to tackle real life issues in a meaningful way (see Chapter Four), and then report results to an audience (see Chapter 11), will be more likely to take great pride in their work and see the joy of learning. Fun comes in many forms. It does not mean that one has to sit and laugh all day. There is a great deal of fun in knowing that you've accomplished a very difficult skill, or in creating new knowledge and reflecting with wisdom on your work (see Chapter Eight). Joy in learning comes from having fun in the process and knowing that you've accomplished something worthwhile. Pride in workmanship is crucial to optimizing learning.

A basic belief of the psychology category of profound knowledge is that everyone comes wanting to do a good job. Do you believe that every student comes to your class wanting to do a good job, and that faulty processes keep everyone from being successful? This is what quality classroom professors believe. I've found this concept to be a difficult one for many to accept.

Motivation of students occurs when:
* they feel respected,
* the professor provides many experiences for decision-making,
* the learning environment is free of fear, and
* learning experiences are meaningful to students.

Pride in workmanship comes from creating products that are meaningful and have a greater audience than the professor. Students who are given roles of equal partners with their classmates and professors will accomplish far more academically than you think possible. Motivation must be internal, rarely external. The carrot and stick approach rarely results in optimizing the achievement.

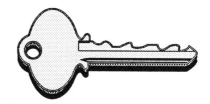

QUALITY BY FACT, OF PROCESS, AND BY PERCEPTION

Everyone examines quality from at least three different perspectives. Each one is important and you must learn to recognize the worth of all three. Each asks a different question of the professor.

* **Quality by fact**—Does the product of the learning experience meet the specified requirements?
* **Quality of process**—Does the process and/or system produce the product as intended?
* **Quality by perception**—Are the customer's expectations met?

Each of these poses an important question for professors. First, quality by fact. Indeed, does the student's work represent quality and does it meet the specifications? This presupposes that you and the students all have a clear understanding of the specified requirements. This goes for every learning experience the students engage in. In later chapters I will examine ways to determine this in detail. Second, quality of the process. The question is: "Does the process allow every student to achieve the learning outcomes intended or are there process flaws?" Last, quality by perception is a major issue in

• When is the last time you did a comprehensive survey of your stakeholders (students, other professors, and employers of your graduates?

• When are you going to do a survey to determine if your class has quality by fact, of process, and by perception?

education today. Many people believe that our educational system is substandard, including those schools and classrooms where students are doing excellent work (and there are many). In many instances we have to overcome the negative attitudes or perceptions of these customers. If your customers believe you have an inferior product, then you will have to deal with this as if it were reality, because it is reality for those customers. In education, you must not only build in quality by fact and process, but you must also deal with the quality by perception issue. You cannot ignore it.

TEACHING AND LEARNING STYLES

Recognition and understanding don't always translate into action, so care must be taken to integrate one's personal preferred teaching style with other teaching styles. Using different teaching styles can be difficult because many of us were reared in an educational system that focused on one method over the others, typically the lecture method.

Imagine a physician who returned from the grave after 100 years and observed an operation. S/he would realize that some sort of healing process was being performed, but s/he would also know that s/he could not take the place of even the nurse. To further illustrate, imagine a manufacturer who returned after 100 years. S/he would not be able to comprehend the production processes now using robotics and statistical process control methods. By the same token, a professor who returned after 100 years would see little difference in how the students were being taught (with the possible exception of technologies) and s/he would not feel uncomfortable in most classroom settings. Just as times have changed in industry and medicine, professors must realize the need for change in classroom strategies.

A quality leader maintains high expectations and uses empowerment methods to gain student commitment to achieving them. S/he recognizes that having high expectations is not enough; one must know how and with what means one can demonstrate and help students achieve them.

This may pose a dilemma for many professors today since an often heard cry is "it takes so much more time and energy." True, quality teaching does take time, especially in the beginning; however, the extra activities you devote yourself to are very different from those in a traditional setting. For instance, a quality professor pays careful attention to the need to show students examples of quality work. Students who have not experienced quality work will have little idea of what it looks like, let alone know how to accomplish quality. This is especially true of individuals who have previously struggled within the traditional top-down boss management style classrooms.

The ability to create initial learning experiences for students that accommodate a variety of learning styles is essential for a quality classroom. To achieve greater knowledge and understanding, it is essential that the professor be able to lead all students into becoming co-producers of additional learning experiences, each one building upon the preceding and accommodating each student's preferred approach to learning. This represents a paradigm shift away from the traditional.

In effect, a quality professor provides the leadership that allows each student to create and successfully carry-out learning, and the professor provides assistance through mentoring, facilitating, and coaching during the learning process. The designated outcomes for each learning experience are established and agreed upon by all; however, the actual way in which the outcomes are reached can be left to the discretion of students and/or teams of students. All this takes place within the broad framework of the course content, but allows for individual differences, student empowerment, and internal motivation.

CONTINUOUS QUALITY IMPROVEMENT (CQI)

Since leadership cannot be sustained without on-going education, it is as important for professors to maintain a high degree of continuous improvement. Continuous improvement comes from reading, attending conferences, seminars, and workshops about quality as well as about one's discipline; keeping active in professional organizations; visiting other colleges and classrooms; and communicating with one's internal and external customers. Engaging in Total Quality obligates the individual to continuously seek out opportunities to provide quality leadership to students and colleagues.

No one ever attains very eminent success by simply doing what is required of him; it is the amount and excellence of what is over and above the required, that determines the greatness of ultimate distinction.
Charles Kendall Adams

Actually, it is difficult to believe that anyone could claim to be a quality leader and not have TQI principles and processes permeate every aspect of his or her life. A quality professor seeks ways to influence others to adopt quality standards. Some obvious ways to do this are through presentations and a willingness to share information and ideas. Another perhaps less obvious way, is to become a better listener. By being an active listener, you send a signal to others of your desire to understand their point of view and their into needs. As Covey (1989) says, seek first to understand, then to be understood. Once you know this, it becomes easier to seek synergism through collaboration and agreement on alternative (win-win) solutions.

Quality professors have an obligation to share their knowledge and leadership with others, but care must be taken not to assume an "air" of superiority when expressing it. Inviting others into your classroom and being open to their ideas, concerns, and suggestions will speak highly of your leadership and knowledge of quality. Sensitivity and patience will be your "friends" as you spread the Quality word.

The classroom leadership role you assume will determine your success as a Quality Professor. Indeed, imagine a classroom where:

- everyone is engaged in meaningful, ability-stretching learning experiences;
- every student knows how to use quality improvement tools to analyze and resolve problems;
- students know how to make the classroom run more efficiently and effectively and how to do their jobs better as they work on improving everyday;
- every student is eager and willing to share information that will help improve the learning experience for everyone;
- every student makes many suggestions for process improvement during the semester and 95% of the suggestions are implemented;
- students work eagerly to resolve real world problems to improve the quality of their life, the life within the community, and the college;
- all students know what is expected of them and that they far exceed the expectations of their parents, the college, and the community;
- students and professors work collaboratively to create a learning environment totally free of fear;
- students and professors experience the joy of learning together daily; and
- students work together in teams and each student contributes to the learning experience.

These are just some of the possible results from creating a quality classroom.

QUALITY IS NOT A MIRACLE

A critic is a man who expects miracles.

James Gibbons Huneker

Using total quality management principles within the classroom is not a quick fix to the myriad of problems we have in colleges today. The technique I am describing is based on using statistics and data to make decisions. It takes time to engage in the Plan-Do-Study-Act cycle, but by examining each process for root causes of problems, you can eliminate them forever as you build quality the teaching/learning system.

A word of caution. You will experience the euphoria of rapid improvement shortly after beginning your quality journey, then things will flatten out. When this happens, what you're really discovering are the beginnings of the root-causing problems underlying the surface problems. Each layer of problem that you uncover will expose another, then another, and another. Each will be more difficult to resolve than the first.

Please be patient when implementing quality. The underlying notion is continuous improvement of every process, and that means that you forgive yourself and the students when mistakes are made. If everyone focuses on continuous improvement, then you can eliminate much of the fear in the classroom. What I suggest is that you remember these things:

- mistakes are opportunities for continuous improvement
- quality is not a miracle;
- quality is a life-long journey—you'll never get there and be able to quit;
- quality is elusive and continues to get better, thus the never-ending journey; and
- quality is what gives us a sense of pride in workmanship.

Create a quality classroom NOW!

ΔΔΔΔΔΔΔΔ

The following is a checksheet tool to help the professor to implement the **Quality Fusion** technique into the classroom.

Step 1: The mission, goals, and academic integrity of your course are absolutely clear.
√   Established a course mission statement.
√   Developed personal goals for the course.
√   Communicated mission and goals to the students.
√   Aligned course mission and goals with those of the department (program/major).

Step 2: You are demonstrating leadership.
√   Developed a definition of a total quality classroom.
√   Walk-the-Talk about quality.
√   Understand Deming's system of **Profound Knowledge**.
√   Use a variety of teaching styles.
√   Have a CQI program for self and for students.

Chapter Three: Most work must be pertinent and flow from the students.

Most of the work professors and students do is best done as teams, flowing from student desire and student concerns. From the beginning the work is infused with student choice, design, revision, execution, reflection and evaluation. Professors are responsible for assessing and ministering to their students' developmental needs.

Most problems that arise during classroom activities are solved in collaboration with students. When a student asks, "Here's a situation that just came up. I don't know what to do about it. What should I do?" the professor turns the question back to the class to wrestle with and solve, rather than simply answering it. Students are trusted continually, and all are led to the point where they welcome responsibility.

By persuading others we convince ourselves.
Junis

BREAKDOWN BARRIERS—DAY 1

Once class begins, start working with the students to establish a mission statement they can understand and "buy into." This essentially answers the WHY question for students. Often students don't know why they have to learn something. If students don't know the answer to the WHY question, they most likely will not be eager participants.

Many students simply will not readily participate unless they understand the relevance to them. These individuals may be reluctant learners. Perhaps you've even called them unmotivated. However, just the opposite is generally true. Students who know the relevance or the WHY of any learning experience are internally motivated learners.

Some professors have a tendency to answer the WHY question by responding with some version of "you'll need to know this when you graduate." That may work for students who have to take a national exam in order to practice their profession, such as nurses, but that doesn't work for too many other students, especially not for those who need more immediate pay-off.

It usually stuns students when professors ask them questions like, "Why are you taking this class?." However, the responses you'll get will tell you a great deal about the way you'll need to work with the class, and even with certain students. In response to the question: WHY ARE YOU HERE? a professor may get a range of answers from:
* my parents made me go to college
* so I can get good grades and go to med school
* so I can get an 'A'
* because I want a degree
* because I want to get a good job

Obviously, you'll want to continue asking WHY until students respond with something about learning. Once they realize they are there to learn, your motivational battles are over. In fact, you cannot motivate students to do anything they don't want to do. To get students beyond the range of answers listed above, you'll want to ask "why" to each of their responses. For instance—If the original answer is "So I can get an 'A'"—ask why do you want/need an 'A'?

STUDENTS AS PARTNERS

Behold, how good and how pleasant it is for brethren to dwell together in unity.

Psalms 133:1

When students have the opportunity to co-create learning experiences with their professor, a higher level of interest, motivation, and achievement results. Given this, it is important to recognize the necessity for professors to shift away from top-down control to full partnerships with students.

While the concept of partnering with students may seem foreign, it is in fact a perfect melding together of notions about teaching and learning. That is, we learn best when we believe the task fulfills a need, is achievable even though it may represent a quantum leap, and will be fun. Otherwise boredom, disinterest, and resistance may result.

If this concept is so obvious, why do so many professors resist changing the instructional format to include students as full partners? One idea may be that we teach the way we were taught, and to date very few colleges are using the "students-as-full-partners" concept.

TEAMING IS A KEY TO QUALITY

One of the first steps you should take is to talk about the concept of teaming with the students. You are setting the stage for the entire semester by letting the students know that each of them is vital to the group and that each is important and has special gifts and skills that others do not have. Include yourself in this discussion as you are a part of this team effort. Set a warm, friendly, classroom climate right away.

Begin the conversation about valuing each other with the fact that there are times when each individual will need help from others and how important it is to know that we all agree to be tutors. Draw some examples from your own college experiences and then ask the students for examples. They may surprise you with the expertise they have already accumulated in this regard.

Engage the students in conversation about teams—what makes a great team, what makes a poor team, etc. Draw examples from baseball, football, basketball, debate, theater performances, etc. Most students can identify or have some ideas about teamwork. From the questions and examples that arise you can easily stimulate discussion about what it takes to have a great team.

You would like the outcome of any discussion about teaming to have the net result of having all students look to each other for help when they require

it and to be supportive of each other. An important concept is that everyone in the course become 'response' 'able' in any given situation. That is, there is a need for everyone (including the professor) to work towards helping move the class forward by not interfering with others' ability to learn, as well as to respond to classmates when they need help. Encourage everyone to engage in the process.

Ask the students for their suggestions about groundrules for engaging in class discussion. The **nominal group process** (NGP) is a good tool to use in this exercise and it is described in the appendix. **Please observe that this point is necessary and without it, your efforts to establish teaming may fail.** This ceremony brings to the forefront those items that are important to each individual. It also helps you to build trust with the students since you are openly discussing the rules by which to manage conflicts. Once the groundrules have been established, make copies and distribute them to each member of the class. Other useful tools to identify and rank problem processes and systems in your classroom are shown in Table 3.1.

As the class works through this exercise, keep in mind that the flow of this class is going to be very different from any the students (or perhaps even you) have experienced before. When the group has established the ground rule(s), you can proceed to the discussion about teaming. This conversation is likely to make some nervous and others may not want to participate. In some instances, students might be more comfortable first discussing this in pairs. Some students will share their previous negative experiences with teams with a friend that they might not share (at first) with the group.

Before the team can begin to collaborate, they will have to understand the "vision" you have in mind for the class. Much of what you are doing is building trust among the students. After all, for many of the students this may be the first time that they will come into contact with others that have widely different cultures, languages, preferences, powers, and yes, even a difference in their beliefs about a deity.

The lack of trust between and among students and professor will be a major factor in determining the overall success of the class. Take it slow, but be persistent. Teaming is an important life-long skill, and one that needs to operate effectively in most jobs.

Trust among students will develop very slowly. Trust among students and professors will also develop more slowly, especially with students who have had negative learning experiences.

The process of gaining students' trust is a slow one. It begins by having the students share some previous experiences with the class. I find it always helps if the professor can share some personal experience that affected attitudes about group work. Sometimes that kind of personal sharing is the thing that can unlock student resistance. You might start by first explaining

TEAMING
Engage your students in a conversation about what makes a good team. Then list examples:

Groundrules for Discussions
Ask your students what the groundrules should be for group discussions. Use the NGP and then list the top five rules.

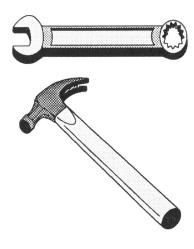

Table 3.1: Several extremely useful total quality improvement tools to identify and rank problem "processes" and/or "systems" in classrooms.

Affinity Diagram
- Used to examine complex and/or hard to understand problems
- Used to build team consensus
- Results can be further analyzed by a Relations Diagram

Cause and Effect Diagram (Fishbones)
- Used to identify root causes of a problem
- Used to draw out many ideas and/or opinions about the causes

Flow Charts
- Give a picture of the processes in the system

Force Field Analysis
- Used when changing the system might be difficult and/or complex

Histogram
- A bar graph of data which displays information about the data set and shape
- Can be used to predict the stability in the system

Nominal Group Process
- A structured process to help groups make decisions
- Useful in choosing a problem to work on
- Used to build team consensus
- Used to draw out many ideas and/or opinions about the causes

Pareto Diagram
- Bar chart that ranks data by categories
- Used to show that a few items contribute greatly to over-all problem(s)
- Helps the team identify which processes/systems to direct their efforts

Relations Diagram
- Helps the team to analyze the cause and effect relationships between complex issues
- Directs the team to the root causes of a problem

Systematic Diagram
- Used when a broad task or goal becomes the focus of the team's work
- Often used after an Affinity Diagram and/or Relations Diagram

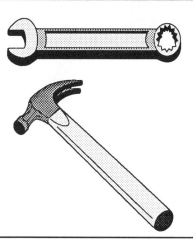

that you know sometimes group work is perceived as too difficult or non-productive, but it is a necessary skill for success in the work force of the 21st century and/or for getting along in families or other groups, and therefore one that will be practiced in your class. You cannot force students to work together, but by continuously focusing on process improvement and improving the classroom culture, most if not all, will eventually come around.

ΔΔΔΔΔΔΔΔΔ

Take a moment and speculate what the top five processes that are in need of improvement in your class. Then take time during the semester and using the NGP technique as described in *The Quality Professor* (1993) ask the students to rank their perceptions about what needs improved.

IDENTIFY THE TOP FIVE PROCESSES THAT ARE IN NEED OF IMPROVEMENT IN YOUR CLASS

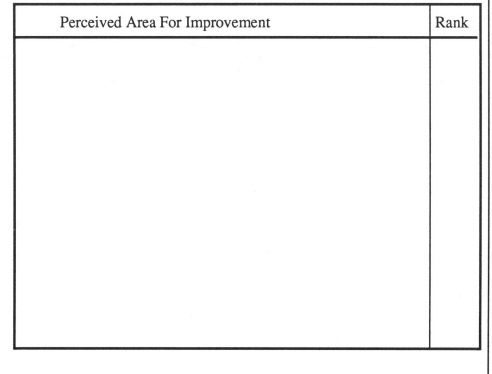

Perceived Area For Improvement	Rank

The **Nominal Group Process** (NGP) can help you identify and rank strengths and weaknesses while giving each participant an equal voice. For the NGP, each group of students should have a facilitator, who acts as a moderator. The facilitator may encourage some members of each team who are reluctant to participate; likewise, the facilitator may restrain members who normally try to control such processes. All members need to feel comfortable with the process and participating in it.

Each group should consist of five to 10 people. Since large classrooms will have several groups, it's possible that each group may perceive different problems/weaknesses. If this should happen, you may have to review the results and plan another session for the entire group before assigning final rankings.

ΔΔΔΔΔΔΔΔ

One effective way of getting the student to begin the buy-in process is simply to ask them to participate. Give a verbal invitation. For reluctant students, you may wish to work through someone who knows that student to make additional contact. Either way, you'll need to make sure that everyone knows:

- the potential benefits;
- what's in it for them and for the class;
- the various connections and expertise that would be available in a team; and,
- the commitment that will be required if they are part of the team.

Of course, they should also be informed that teaming has the potential to produce problems—but I suggest that you minimize the negative aspects about teaming and inform them that as problems arise you and the class will handle them.

One of the problems that is constantly brought out by the students is the "Lack of Communication" between team members. I suggest that you acknowledge this potential problem by pointing out that when two people communicate, two communication pathways exist: one from person A who communicates to person B; and the second from person B who communicates to person A. However, when three people communicate, six pathways exist as shown in the following figure:

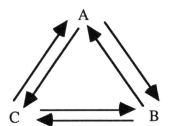

Then, to emphasize the importance of teamwork and communication, I suggest you introduce the formula for the number of pathways which is: N (N-1). Therefore, when 3 people are in a group, they will have 3(3-1) = 3(2) or 6 communication pathways. So with a team of nine people, they will have 9(8) or 72 communication pathways.

STUDENTS AS PROBLEM SOLVERS

One approach to teaming is to share a problem-solving model with the students. This means that each team understands that (just like in the real-world) there may be times when people don't communicate properly and the job isn't getting done. In this case, as in all others, the group has to take responsibility for resolving any problems. Thus, the professor's role changes from boss-manager to mentor and facilitator. Students can and should be responsible for working through most classroom problems.

One way to approach this is to educate students about one of the many problem-solving models. One possible model might very well consist of the following steps:

Step 1:   A problem is identified by either the professor or someone in the class.

Step 2:   A convener is chosen to select a team to address the problem.

Step 3:   A meeting is held.

Step 4:   The problem is clearly stated.

Step 5:   Facts are separated from fiction and self-interests are disclosed.

Step 6:   Solutions are brainstormed (without judgment).

Step 7:   Consequences of each solution are considered.

Step 8:   Decision for change is made and results are recorded.

Classes which are taught and regularly practice something like this model are more successful at staying focused on the task and get the "job" done with minimal problems. These are classrooms where students function quite nicely while the professor is working with an individual or another team. The students do not require constant supervision. In fact, the more students practice their own problem solving, the more empowered they become, thus leading to greater self-confidence and sense of responsibility for their own behavior.

Other ways to engage students as problem solvers include the use of quality improvement tools such as the Cause & Effect Diagram, Relations Diagram, and the Force Field Analysis—these and other tools and techniques are described in *The Quality Professor* (1993).

Once to every man and nation comes the moment to decide, In strife of Truth and Falsehood, for the good or evil side;
J.R. Lowell

WHAT IS QUALITY?

One of the first steps in working with students is to discuss the question of quality. What does quality mean to them? Can they also specify factors that are involved in their notion of quality? The answer is a resounding YES! Not only can students understand the concept of quality, they are eager to tell you.

Whenever you engage students in a study around a quality framework, the interest levels will remain high. What is meant by a quality framework?

Simply put, the students have to understand what quality is, and how it will be determined.

ΔΔΔΔΔΔΔΔ

Take a moment and compare your answers to the following questions to those of your students.

What is the difference between product quality and product features?

How can you and every student in your class be engaged in quality control?

What are some of the quality improvement tools and techniques that can be used in the problem solving model mentioned above to measure increased quality of product and/or service?

ΔΔΔΔΔΔΔΔ

QUALITY FACTORS!

It may be necessary to explain quality factors. **Quality Factors are measurable!** They are product specifications that must be met before either a student or a team is granted an acknowledgment for having mastered the competencies and/or skills of your course. As students gain this concept they learn that **quality factors are product specifications for each learning experience**. These are the fundamentals that will ultimately determine whether or not they have achieved quality. Students quickly learn that the only acceptable outcome of any learning experience is quality.

OPERATIONAL DEFINITIONS

The next obvious question is what has to either transpire or go into the learning experience (product) to create quality? Explain to the students that they are creating **operational definitions** for making the learning experience. If the operational definitions are not followed carefully, then the results will be less than the best.

An operational definition is a very precise statement of what is expected to create a quality factor. An operational definition is a prerequisite for collecting data and evaluating results, therefore, every member of your class must understand every operational definition. Operational definitions are appropriate for every process or system that is to be improved as well as for every quality factor to be obtained.

NOTE

By going through the aforementioned recommendations, your students will quickly have grasped the significance of the mission statements, teaming, PDCA cycle, variation, quality factors (course specifications or competencies), and operational definitions (the steps that have to be taken and/or the things that have to transpire) to demonstrate that the quality factors have been obtained. Consequently students will be able to start your class learning about quality and CQI principles, in addition to the content of your course, be it either chemistry or art. This sets the stage for quality learning experiences and achieves them in a way that is both entertaining and fun yet makes the point very clearly.

Operational Definitions

• Are very precise statements of what is expected from a process

• Are appropriate for every process or system to be improved

• Must be accepted by the professor and by the students of the quality improvement team

• Are flexible and can be changed if the process or system is changed

---

PERTINENT WORK AND INTERDISCIPLINARY ACTIVITIES

What is pertinent work and how can it be achieved in any classroom? Pertinent work must include learning fundamentals, but it is the "how" that can be negotiated and collaboratively determined by students and professors. For example, when teaching "Environmental Science" to freshman Biology Majors, it might be better if you create a joint venture with professors in Speech, English, and, say, Economics so that these students could **speak** on environmental issues, **write** on environmental issues, and measure the impact **economically** on environmental issues. This would mean, however, that the students and the professors would have to coordinate their schedules if such a cooperative learning experience were to be established.

One successful adventure occurred in the laboratory science courses at California State University in Bakersfield. Under the leadership of Jack Coash, Dean of Natural Sciences and Mathematics, "Inquiry Learning" was introduced under a National Science Foundation grant. Teams of students would determine a laboratory project that they wanted to do over the semester. The projects were pertinent to their major or interests. For example, in the

"General Microbiology" course, a group of nursing students chose to examine the number of air borne bacteria in hospital rooms before and during the making of beds. Another group of premedical students tested the antibacterial effectiveness of various mouthwashes by taking cultures before and after gargling for various periods of time. A group of environmental science majors determined the number of coliform bacteria in various streams as a function of rain and temperature. One of my favorites is a group of art majors who wanted to "paint" the soil. They permeated canvases with various types of selective media and then sprinkled various soil samples over the canvas. They incubated the canvases in their bathrooms under high humidity conditions. The growth consisted of various molds and bacteria of various colors—each was unique. They preserved their "art" with hair spray and displayed it at a regional art show where they won first prize! Regardless of their projects all groups had to learn the basics of sterile techniques, plate counts, dilutions, use of the microscopes, staining, preparation of selective media, etc., prior to getting their project approved by the professor.

In preparing some kind of classroom experience that will encompass interdisciplinary activities and relate directly to the specified competency of your course, your students will need to know what is expected of them.

- **Why are we doing this?** The reason must be compelling for everyone, otherwise they will not "buy in" and will resist teaming efforts. I recommend that the goals for each learning experience be written collaboratively with students and professor and posted in the classroom. The goals can also be written with the quality factors and operational definitions.

- **What are the quality factors we will look for? How will we assess our results?** Limit the quality factors to the top two or three. Be certain to work with the students so everyone understands that these are the ways their work will be judged, and that once they achieve the quality factors, they can move on to other things, but that everyone must reach quality. Here you can emphasize the importance of working together. This will be discussed in detail in another chapter. As students progress, a quality factor you might want to routinely include is **cycle time**. That is, how much time will be given to any learning experience? A quality classroom seeks to continually improve the learning experiences while reducing cycle time. Thus students advance more rapidly in a quality classroom.

- **Create operational definitions. If you were going to tell someone specifically how to create "an excellent oil painting," what would you say?** What are the key elements or ingredients that are necessary to achieve the "best?" Beginning art students will need more guidance than senior art majors. Begin by seeding the list with one or two obvious particulars and then allow the students to come up with others. You'll need to guide them through this, particularly when first starting the continuous quality improvement process. If the students don't come up with all the fundamentals (or learning objectives) then you should add to the list by stating that you are a part of the group, too. For that reason, you are adding these elements. Once this is fully developed and understood by all, post the operational definitions along with the quality factors and mission statement.

People seldom improve when they have no other model but themselves to copy.
Goldsmith

ΔΔΔΔΔΔΔΔΔ

For each process that was targeted for improvement, complete the following form.

PROCESS IMPROVEMENT GUIDE
Quality Improvement Team Leader:_____ Date: _____
Mission Statement:
Quality Factors (What are the goals?)
Operational Definitions (What is necessary to achieve the Quality Factors?

ΔΔΔΔΔΔΔΔ

ELIMINATE CONFUSION

Prior to beginning any learning experience then, students are given a copy of the Mission, Quality Factors, and Operational Definitions. This **eliminates any confusion** that might arise about the assignment or requirements.

By reaching into your own experiences, you might be able to plant thought seeds of creativity for learning experiences. Begin with something exciting and not too complex, but that everyone can relate to.

Wouldn't it be fascinating to study the economics of either an environmental issue or a health issue and how it might affect the local economy as well as the state, region, or national economies?

The learning outcomes that an be generated from the question(s) are limitless. Imagine the reading, writing, research, speaking, listening skills involved. Imagine the data gathering, charting and graphing, statistical analysis and other mathematical skills that can be learned. Imagine the scientific discovery methods, problem solving, critical thinking, and new knowledge possibilities. Students majoring in Mass Media or Communications can create brochures, write newspaper articles, hold press conferences, lobby their state and national legislators, and testify before public groups. They may even want to team up with a national organization interested in saving the planet. With an interdisciplinary approach, students can learn a phenomenal amount, maintain a high degree of motivation, achieve far beyond their expectations, and maybe most important, will feel empowered that they've done something significant; that the assignment was not merely "work" from a textbook, but truly significant.

When an assignment is completed, and the quality factors are met, students and professor debrief. Here is one example of a simple debriefing form after a learning experience.

How Helpful Were These Resources?

Class _____   Semester_____

Period_____   Project _____

For this competency, we used the following resources:

Lecture   Field Trip
Textbooks   Video
Library books   Computers
Discussion   Other
Newspaper - Magazine Articles

Please rate each on how much it helped you complete the learning experience:
E = excellent, couldn't have completed it without it.
G = good; was a big help
O = okay; didn't help much
W = waste of time; was no help whatsoever

	RATING			
Method	E	G	O	W
Lecture				
Textbooks				
Library Books				
Discussion				
Articles				
Field Trip				
Video				
Computers				
Other				

What suggestions do you have for improving this learning experience?

When students have completed the debriefing sheet, the quality team or professor can collate the responses by using the debriefing check sheet. This information can improve all subsequent learning experiences. For example, if 40% of all students rated the lectures "okay", while an equal percentage rated them good or excellent, you would want to pursue with the students what was helpful and what wasn't. Many of us identify with our work and become defensive when students offer criticism or make suggestions. I caution you to resist doing that when you ask students to help. If you ask and they are honest, which is what you hope for, then don't become defensive. Ask for help and be grateful when it comes. In this case the lectures may require some alteration to become more effective for all the students.

If, for example, over 40% of students think the textbook is a waste while 45% were lukewarm about its worth, you might either want to change textbooks or limit the required reading. Don't ignore what the students have said. They will continue to view you with goodwill as long as they can see that their suggestions are being taken seriously and changes are being made.

Keep the course mission statement in the forefront of your mind throughout these experiences. Remember that every action taken within the classroom should support the mission statement and goals.

Other ways to debrief after any learning experience are discussed in another chapter. The above method may be helpful to professors as they proceed on their own continuous improvement journey.

CLASSROOM DISSENSION
More traditional professors become uncomfortable when problems arise within the classroom. However, by focusing on the process rather than the outcome, the entire class can come together to resolve almost any problem. Generally when students are encouraged to resolve their own problems, the result is far superior and more long-lasting than if problems are resolved from other sources. This is an important point for quality professors and one that totally requires the belief that all students want to do a good job, but that it is the system that keeps them (and the professor) from being successful.

FINALLY...
Quality classrooms are distinguishable in several ways. Professors engage students continuously in co-creating the learning experiences. Work that is assigned has meaning to the students and real-world connections. Each learning experience grows upon the others and results from students and professor debriefing and analyzing the previous assignment before creating the next.

Professors in quality classrooms do not resolve problems in isolation but they work together with students, knowing that the collective wisdom of the group is much greater than their own. Students become empowered, more self-confident, eager life-long learners who care about the class as a whole and are willing to assist others as needed.

Responsibility for learning rests with each student, the teams, and with the class as a whole including the professor. Everyone contributes to expanding the thinking of the group and works together to create exciting, efficient learning experiences.

ΔΔΔΔΔΔΔΔΔ

The following is a checksheet tool to help the professor to implement the **Quality Fusion** technique into the classroom.

Step 1: The mission, goals, and academic integrity of your course are absolutely clear.
- √ Established a course mission statement.
- √ Developed personal goals for the course.
- √ Communicated mission and goals to the students.
- √ Aligned course mission and goals with those of the department (program/major).

Step 2: You are demonstrating leadership.
- √ Developed a definition of a total quality classroom.
- √ Walk-the-Talk about quality.
- √ Understand Deming's system of **Profound Knowledge**.
- √ Use a variety of teaching styles.
- √ Have a CQI program for self and for students.

Step 3: All work is pertinent and flows from the students.
- √ Broke down barriers on day one by establishing a course mission statement with the students.
- √ Had students co-create learning experiences.
- √ Stressed the importance of teamwork in problem solving and decision making.
- √ Defined quality and what it means.
- √ Created interdisciplinary learning activities.

Chapter Four: Course content is connected to the campus community and the real world.

One of the most common complaints students have about most course work is that it lacks relevance to their lives and world. Students interviewed about their future rarely say they believe what they are learning in general education courses has any relationship to their future career plans. We all know that when presented with something we are not interested in, there is little incentive to learn about it. No matter how much someone tries to convince us, if we cannot imagine that it will add any value to our lives, we simply reject it. Occasionally, someone with great influence over us can persuade us to try something. Sad to say, that is rarely the case between students and their professors outside of their major. An excellent professor may be able to persuade some of the students to become involved because s/he works so hard at making "it" interesting. However, far too many professors become burned out, while far too many students still see no added value to the subject matter. Thus, we are left with professors viewing students as unmotivated and not interested in learning.

If we carefully examine this phenomena, however, a different picture emerges. It is human nature to continue learning. Humans are very complex. We spend our days learning new skills and abilities that we believe will bring us respect, love, survival, happiness, and fun. As we grow and develop, we learn to act and react to outside influences (usually significant others) who give us feedback on our behaviors. The need to love and be loved, and the need for respect become the core of what drives our behavior. Thus, by the time a youngster reaches college, behavior patterns are well established, based on the reaction of parents/guardians, grandparents, siblings, etc.

Students don't lose their enthusiasm for learning—they simply lose their enthusiasm for being told what to learn, when to learn it, how to learn it, and where to learn it. Students who appear unmotivated in class are seldom 'vegetables' who sit in front of the television. They are often very active learners outside of class, but are not afforded the opportunity to learn in ways that meet their preferred learning styles. In fact, we penalize students whose learning styles are a mismatch with our preferred teaching style.

The interesting thing about teaching and learning styles is that you may be teaching, but some students are not learning because it is like a foreign language if they are not tuned into your style. Sadly, these students get further behind and are often punished for something over which they have no control. These are the students who have so many failures that they are stripped of their self-esteem and drop out of college.

What looks like a unmotivated student is really a student who has been denied the right to learn in ways that are interesting and exciting to him/her.

I believe there is no such thing as an unmotivated learner. But rather many students are no longer motivated to be compliant in a system that does not recognize their worth as individuals. One glance at students when they are out of class reveals that they are continuously learning. Unfortunately, many are learning behaviors and other things that we wish they wouldn't.

One thing is very clear: Most students start college eager to learn. By the time they reach the second semester, many say they hate, not dislike, but HATE college. They respond to a system they view as uncaring by not caring since it probably hurts less that way. Students make a very strong statement that the system has failed by virtue of their behaviors. Absenteeism, tardiness, disrespect for professors are all expressions of dissatisfaction with the system.

If you have a sense that students are not responding enthusiastically to an assignment that you have poured your heart and soul into, then the first thing to do is ask the students to analyze the problem for you. Approach it from the perspective that you need their help since you cannot figure out why they are still unresponsive to the wonderful assignments.

ATTACH THE LEARNING EXPERIENCE
It is absolutely crucial to attach every learning experience to the student's world. You can do this three ways:
1) Based on the required and recommended competencies, have students consider ways they would like to learn so you can co-create the learning experiences together.
2) Interact with colleagues and create a cross-curricular approach to learning, thus making each learning experience meaningful to the students. "Learning Communities," in my opinion, will become the teaching/learning system of the future.
3) Be prepared to answer the WHY question, as it relates to why students need to learn your subject matter, and be certain to ask students WHY they are in your class.

Quality professors are much better at engaging in cross-curricular activities ("Learning Communities") than average professors. It makes sense to approach learning holistically rather than in isolation as it most often is presented.

For example, have you ever encountered a math problem that was just a series of numbers completely unattached to "something?" Think about the folly of teaching this way. Mathematics and the logic underlying it should become a part of all education, not just reserved for 50 minutes per class on Monday, Wednesday, and Friday. The same can be said for communication skills, science, and even physical education.

Have you ever considered how much physical education relies on the principles of anatomy, physiology, psychology, mathematics, physics, geometry, and kinesiology? Yet, there are not many attempts to integrate this into most physical education courses. Interestingly, we consider book learning to be academic, but applied knowledge is often viewed as vocational. Without application, what is the lesson to be learned?

Even Shakespeare and other masters' works can be taught so that there is meaning for each student's life. The classics are the author's way of problem resolution, and classics deal with situations that are still happening to students today. Humanity is still fraught with inequity, and there are abundant examples throughout the great works of literature.

Therefore, whatever your subject matter, your curricular interests, you must work from the supposition that it can be brought to the student's world, and thus increase their motivation to learn and at the same time decrease drop-out rates.

> Doing more of what you've always done will get you more of what you've always gotten. The question is: Are all the students being successful and are they all internally motivated to do high quality work?

ΔΔΔΔΔΔΔΔΔ

The following is a checksheet tool to help the professor to implement the **Quality Fusion** technique into the classroom.

Step 1:   The mission, goals, and academic integrity of your course are absolutely clear.

√   Established a course mission statement.
√   Developed personal goals for the course.
√   Communicated mission and goals to the students.
√   Aligned course mission and goals with those of the department (program/major).

Step 2:   You are demonstrating leadership.
√   Developed a definition of a total quality classroom.
√   Walk-the-Talk about quality.
√   Understand Deming's system of **Profound Knowledge**.
√   Use a variety of teaching styles.
√   Have a CQI program for self and for students.

Step 3:   All work is pertinent and flows from the students.
√   Broke down barriers on day one by establishing a course mission statement with the students.
√   Had students co-create learning experiences.
√   Stressed the importance of teamwork in problem solving and decision making.
√   Defined quality and what it means.
√   Created interdisciplinary learning activities.

Step 4:   The course content is connected to the surrounding community and the real world.
√   Demonstrated the connectedness between work and the real world.
√   Asked the students to analyze the learning assignments.
√   Began TQM training for the students.
√   Implemented student suggestions on how best to improve the learning system.

Chapter Five: **The student is not only treated as a "worker," but also as a team member of the "research and development" department.**

Traditionally the college professor lectures while the students take notes. The students are passive learners.

More progressive professors do vary their teaching styles and attempt to make the subject matter interesting; however, far too many still adhere to the strict lecture method.

Professors have become boxed into their particular subject matter, partly because of scheduling but also because their paradigm is that classes are separate entities with little or no reason to interact with colleagues. Some colleges have included a teaming in the classrooms, but only a few are also using an interdisciplinary approach, called "Learning Communities," to learning.

The paradigm shift of applying TQM to the teaching/learning system is so dramatic that professors, administrators, and parents all have difficulty conceptualizing what a quality college or classroom would be like. The basic problem is that everyone was schooled in a very traditional way, and grandparents were schooled the same way, too. Unless each individual can think differently about education, the tendency will be to continue to re-create a poor system.

STUDENTS AS WORKERS

One aspect of the great paradigm shift for professors is in the way students are viewed. Releasing oneself from the traditional view of students is critical to make the shift to quality. This is not to be taken lightly and must be considered carefully. In quality systems, students are viewed as both primary customers and workers within the system. In this chapter, I put the " student-as-worker" and the "professor-as-the-classroom-manager" concept on center stage. That is, students are expected to perform the assignments or the work within the processes leading to the system the professor has created.

To my mind the best investment a young man starting out in business could possibly make is to give all his time, all his energies to work, just plain, hard work.
C.M. Schwab

Below are flow charts showing an assignment in a traditional classroom.

Figure 5.1: Process and Deployment Flow Charts of a typical classroom assignment.

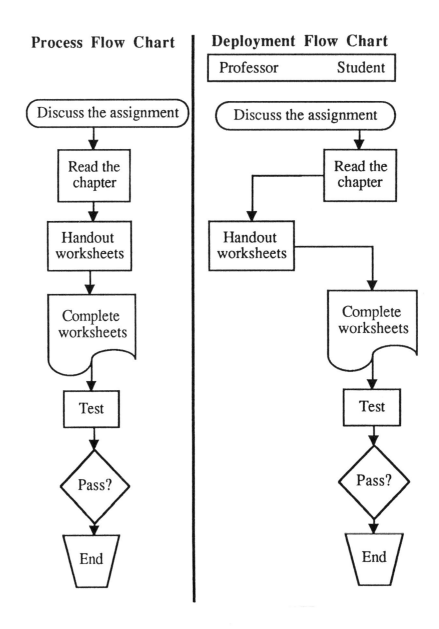

You can see from the flow charts that there is no room in the processes within this system for students to evaluate their activities or the way they are supposed to achieve the end product which, in this case, is to pass the test after having mastered the material. Consequently, if there is a mismatch between teaching and learning styles, a student in this class will be unable to function optimally. If the materials are not adequate, students will be unable to achieve optimally. If the assignment does not have relevance to the student's world, or if s/he doesn't understand how learning this particular skill fits into his/her future, the student will have little incentive to conceptualize and assimilate the material. None of the above is an indictment of the professor, but rather each represents system flaws that could be resolved with input from the workers. Deming and other quality experts believe that workers (down on the factory floor—*i.e.*, those working within the system) are in the best position to make suggestions for improvement. Since students are the ones who must produce assignments within the rules that are controlled by the professor, it is not unreasonable to view them as workers within the classroom system.

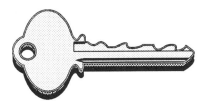

△△△△△△△△△
Take several minutes and reflect on the following fundamental principles of TQM/CQI. Then describe your personal beliefs underneath each tenet.

Fundamental Principles to the TQM/CQI Philosophy
Do you believe when a student can't learn and when you were not able to help him/her, there was a process problem in the system, and as a result, you, as the manager, will have to remove the process problem, i.e., the root cause?   My personal belief statement:
Do you believe that the professor is most knowledgeable about his/her job?   My personal belief statement:
Do you believe that everyone wants to do their job well and to feel like a valuable contributor?   My personal belief statement:
Do you believe that more can be accomplished by working together as a team to improve the system, rather than having individuals working to get around the system?   My personal belief statement:
Do you believe that structured problem-solving techniques, using graphs, and statistical charts are much better than an unstructured process as they point out areas where improvements are most likely to be effective?   My personal belief statement:
Do you believe that adversarial relationships between professor and the students, or professor and management are counterproductive?   My personal belief statement:

If you have little disagreement with the dogmas, you are well under way to successfully implementing TQM/CQI in your classes.

ΔΔΔΔΔΔΔΔ

STEPS TO SYSTEM IMPROVEMENT

I suggest that you begin your course with an introduction to quality management theory. The conversation can begin with a historical overview of Dr. Deming and the other quality leaders, or that can take place later. This overview is necessary because students need to realize why you have chosen to do things differently. Everyone over 30 can understand the story about Japan and the products they produced as being junk. But what about students today? For the most part, they grew up in a world where Japanese products have been revered for their quality, reliability, and technology. Few students can recall when Japanese products were considered inferior, so the brief history lesson about quality is important.

Along with that, I recommend a brief discussion about what has happened in our country with our major corporations. Some students, perhaps not the youngest, can relate very well to stories about the auto industry, television, video games, computer chips, etc. If you are unfamiliar with these stories, do some research. Students will be fascinated (depending on the way you tell the stories) and many can relate because their parents may work for one of those companies, or may work in a retail store that sells televisions, etc. You'll need to put the quality story into context for the youth so that they can link the information to their own lives.

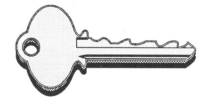

Follow this discussion with a general conversation about quality and what it means to do quality work. Then, move the students into a discussion about things that make it easier to learn and things that make it more difficult. You may get some excellent clues right away from the students as to what can be done to help make it better. Let the students know that you are serious about asking them for help. You might want to talk about an experience you had in school where no matter how hard you tried, you just couldn't understand something.

Sometimes professors are afraid to ask students for help because they think the students will turn on them. Perhaps they are more afraid that they will *hear*, perhaps for the first time, that they are not a success. This must be tied to professors' fear of evaluation. We have put professors in the position of being the "expert" for so long, that it is frightening for them to think that they may not know all the answers.

In a quality classroom, action is rarely if ever taken without first analyzing root causes of problems and embarking on a plan-do-check-act (PDCA) cycle for process improvement.

> **To improve the systems in the class the professor must:**
>
> 1. **Concentrate on improving processes**
>
> 2. **Use a plan-do-check-act (PDCA) cycle**
>
> 3. **Use a variety of quality improvement tools and techniques**

Given this, what part does the student as worker play in the scheme of a quality classroom? The learning experiences in a quality classroom are characterized by student action, rather than passive receipt of processed information. Students are continually led into new work and unfamiliar territory. Once skills are "won," they must be reapplied to new problems in new ways.

In this configuration, students always operate at the edge of their competence. Therefore, it must be clear to them that a mistake is not a failure, but an attempt at innovation. They must realize that positive, constructive scrutiny of those mistakes by the rest of the class can only occur in an atmosphere free of fear where students never have to risk embarrassment.

Trust and respect remain the foundation upon which a Quality Classroom can be built. If the foundation is weak, progress will be sporadic and lead to frustration, and eventually the disenfranchised students will opt out.

> **A Quality Classroom cannot be built in an atmosphere of distrust.**

Trust within the classroom means students can:
- Take "learning" risks without fear of being shamed
- Express their opinions about the learning experience without fear of being punished, ridiculed, or ignored
- Be responsible for solving problems
- Focus on learning without a coercive atmosphere

Trust within the classroom means professors can:
- Allow students to co-create the learning environment and learning experiences
- Release the "need" to control
- Focus on leadership
- Develop and use students' problem solving skills so more time can be spent learning
- Seek data from internal and external customers freely and use it as a basis for improvement

Fear is an overwhelming issue for all students, and the more fear invades the classroom, the less willing the students will be to work together. Building trust among students isn't as easy as it might seem. Bias and prejudice are factors that must be overcome also. Students who have experienced put downs are going to be understandably less willing to take risks than others.

I am not suggesting that every learning experience has to be a team

effort, but that teaming become a routine part of education. There can and should be opportunities for students to engage in individual research as well, and the two experiences need not be at odds with each other.

WHAT ABOUT STUDENTS WHO REFUSE TO PARTICIPATE?

You will undoubtedly find situations where some students simply refuse to work with others. These may be students who present themselves as being "tough." These situations always present a dilemma to professors.

Patience and understanding are your biggest allies. I recommend that you find ways to develop a rapport and see if they'll eventually share with you some of the reasons for not wanting to team. Whatever you do, **never** embarrass or humiliate a student. It will be nearly impossible for you to establish a good rapport and engage him/her as part of the team or class because s/he simply won't trust you.

Patience is the art of hoping.
French proverb

You can engage some of the more reluctant students more readily when you have students solve problems as a group.

As in all learning experiences, allow time to reflect and debrief after every group exercise. Students may not be used to having reflective time, or time to talk about the problems they encountered and how they would improve the process if there were time to repeat it. The debriefing sessions are as valuable as the actual activity. You are establishing a ritual for the class to follow as you move through the semester. You'll want students to feel comfortable expressing their opinions in an effort to improve every single process. This is a key factor in engaging students as research and development experts. In essence, you are asking them to portray that role every time you debrief and engage in the Plan-Do-Check-Act cycle.

ΔΔΔΔΔΔΔΔΔ

The following is a checksheet tool to help the professor to implement the **Quality Fusion** technique into the classroom.

Step 1: The mission, goals, and academic integrity of your course are absolutely clear.
    √ Established a course mission statement.
    √ Developed personal goals for the course.
    √ Communicated mission and goals to the students.
    √ Aligned course mission and goals with those of the department (program/major).

Step 2: You are demonstrating leadership.
    √ Developed a definition of a total quality classroom.
    √ Walk-the-Talk about quality.
    √ Understand Deming's system of **Profound Knowledge**.
    √ Use a variety of teaching styles.
    √ Have a CQI program for self and for students.

Step 3: All work is pertinent and flows from the students.
    √ Broke down barriers on day one by establishing a course mission statement with the students.
    √ Had students co-create learning experiences.
    √ Stressed the importance of teamwork in problem solving and decision making.
    √ Defined quality and what it means.
    √ Created interdisciplinary learning activities.

Step 4: The course content is connected to the surrounding community and the real world.
    √ Demonstrated the connectedness between work and the real world.
    √ Asked the students to analyze the learning assignments.
    √ Began TQM training for the students.
    √ Implemented student suggestions on how best to improve the learning system.

Step 5: The student is treated as a "worker," but s/he is also considered a valuable team member of the "research and development" department.
    √ Gave the students an historical overview about the quality movement and discussed examples.
    √ Discussed the P-D-C-A cycle and root causes of problems.

Chapter Six: Peer teaching, small group work, and team work are emphasized.

In quality classrooms, students and the professor view themselves as part of the larger group. Everyone has a sense of the need to work together and help each other. The concept of cheating doesn't exist since everyone is working towards gaining more knowledge and combining it with existing knowledge to create new knowledge. Students are led by their professor and classmates to know where and how to access information which becomes more important than memorizing facts.

There is less misery in being cheated than in that kind of wisdom which perceives, or thinks it perceives, that all mankind are cheats.
E.H. Chapin

One must be careful not to imagine that some base knowledge is not important, because it is crucial and provides the foundation upon which all future knowledge is born. However, the way this material is presented and learned is different. Rote memorization is seldom useful. This might cause some discomfort to those more traditional professors who believe that certain things like historical dates must be memorized. Consider that most information can be gleaned from using a dictionary, a calculator, a map, or a book. Doesn't it truly make more sense to have students learn to use the tools of learning that can open up the entire universe to them as they need it, rather than have them memorize some facts to store in their short-term memory to regurgitate on a test?

What changes in the quality classroom is the WHY question. Students and professors must understand why they are being asked to learn something, and if it has no meaning in their lives, they probably will resist learning it. Some students, those who are vested in pleasing adults, will go along with whatever the professor asks, but even these students have trouble recalling facts that have not been placed in context or learned in the context of some assignment with meaning.

A key element of a quality classroom is engaging students to help make the learning fun! Professors know the intended outcomes, and students know what makes learning fun! Why not combine the expertise of all and seek help from students as to how best to learn something.

Here is an excellent example of how one academic department and a professor in Arizona answers the WHY question. Let's look at sections taken from the department's "**Orientation**" manual and her syllabus.

Do you have an orientation manual and/or training session for all students in your classes? If you do, please take time to outline what is covered in your training sessions.

Understand what the Biology Department expects of you and what you can expect of us.
- **How to do it vs. What to do**
- **Specific Examples**
- **Stress Outcomes**

What is the ultimate goal of your class? (If it is to improve the learning environment, do your students know it?) What is the main focus of your class? What makes your class unique?

Understand the Biology's Department ultimate goal is to improve student LEARNING.

- **We create learning experiences related to real world experiences.**
- **It is our main focus**
- **It is our uniqueness**
- **It is our positioning**
- **Service drives our entire operation**
- **It is our HIGHEST MISSION**

What are the values and philosophy of your class?

Class Values and Philosophy

I believe in Our Students, the most important part of our institution. I will operate the Class so that I provide our students with top quality facilities and services. Students are my greatest resource and I will treat my students in all classes with fairness and respect. My Class tradition: In all we do we strive to be the best.

What is the credo (belief system) of your classes? Is it known to your students?

My Classroom Credo

My classroom is a place where the genuine care and learning environment of my students is my highest mission. I pledge to provide the finest personal service for my students, who will always find a friendly, warm and yet, refined atmosphere.

Do you empower your students? If so, explain.

You are the Expert

Be aware of events and things the we are doing in the Course. Inform people about activities in all areas. This not only makes good conversation, but it also makes them feel good about the College. Be aggressive about sharing that information with other people.

Anticipate Needs

Stop to help people who look like they need help and go beyond the minimum expectations. Help those with a bewildered look on their face. Remember, it is not cheating to help another person learn.

Measure and Monitor Learning
- **Student Comments**
- **Rating Cards**
- **Focus Groups**
- **Ask Students What I Can Do Better**

Do you empower your students to gather customer satisfaction data about your teaching and/or learning environment? Please explain.

To be Successful and Keep Your Sanity
- **You need to genuinely like people**
- **You need to like working and serving people**
- **You need to accept the challenge**

Do your students like to serve people and have fun while they are doing it? If yes, please describe and give examples. If no, how do you intend to get rid of the pre-med syndrome?

NEVER A NEVER & NEVER AN ALWAYS

I **don't** suggest students always work in teams because there is great benefit to learning to work independently as well. It is crucial that students also learn to follow a task through from start to finish. Some very, very bright students have so many creative thoughts running through their heads that sometimes they are unable to focus on anything long enough to complete a task. Learning to follow-through and accomplish the goal is vital to success in life. Therefore, I recommend professors find a way to mix the learning experiences so that students spend part of each day working independently from a team or partner.

Independent work does not mean that you abandon the idea of peer teaching, having fun, or working on meaningful experiences.

ASSESSMENT

Individual learning experiences can also be integrated with peer teaching and pairing. Part of this experience is teaching students to assess their work as well as the work of their peers. Assessing truly is an art, and one that requires facilitation and mentoring by the professor. Students often can be cruel with those they somehow view as "less" bright than they. This can become a difficult and tricky issue, and one that requires a great deal of sensitivity for

One of life's most painful moments comes when we must admit that we didn't do our homework, that we are not prepared.
                    Merlin Olsen

professor and students.

Peer assessment and/or self-assessment are skills that can be taught, and once implemented, can yield great rewards for students. However, you must realize that if the students have any fears of receiving a lower grade because of self-assessment it will be impossible for them to be honest in their assessment. Analysis of this makes perfect sense, since we generally do not willingly engage in things that we know will bring harm to us.

It is not difficult to imagine the sensitivity that must be used when broaching the subject of self-assessment and peer assessment. However, it is a key concept in a quality classroom due to the vast advantages that can derive from its use. For example, students who can assess their work demonstrate a tremendous ability to know how much more is required of them to complete the task. These students work on the concept of continuous improvement and are not concerned when others complete the task sooner. Furthermore, when students become comfortable with their peers assessing their work, they soon realize how important and valuable it is to gain feedback from another person. Too often, especially in writing assignments, the writer has difficulty viewing his work from another perspective. By using peer and self-assessment techniques, we can move students forward in creating much more refined works.

Sometimes peer assessment can split the class if some students decide to be particularly harsh when assessing classmates' work. Realistically, we have to recognize that some students may have received ill treatment from their peers. That's why it is important to give whatever time it takes to teach students ways to assess others' work without making personal attacks on each other.

The next step is to provide everyone with some guidelines for assessing each other's work. The best way to keep peer assessment out of the personal realm is to remind students of the operational definitions and quality factors already agreed upon by the group. Use those as the rubric guide.

There really shouldn't be any questions (not many for certain) because the operational definitions must be measurable. For example: *The use of good paragraphs* is not an operational definition since "good paragraph" cannot be measured. How would one know necessarily what a good paragraph was except to mentally take a paragraph apart and analyze it. The result of your analysis does create operational definitions.

The class will be able to do this, but you may need to prompt them somewhat in the beginning. We suggest that after students complete the peer assessment rubric, they write some comments and suggestions for improvement. After, provide time for peers to reflect with their partner about the comments and rubric. This can be the most valuable part of the experience. Students learn excellent communication skills, and they also become mentors for their partner. It is this synergy of students working together to help each other make greater gains than they could have gotten independently that is so exciting for students and the teacher. Indeed, the reward of using this approach is not simply that individual students make greater gains, it is in seeing how students come to value each other in completely different ways. They begin to view each other as resources other than for social events.

To facilitate this process, it is a good idea to generate some samples and have students practice. Your samples can become more complex as students have had practice with the more obviously flawed one(s). After each practice run, engage students in a conversation about how they've scored it and the comments made. Have them compare responses and provide samples until students become familiar with the format and begin to get consensus on scoring. Always remember to review the operational definitions prior to giving out the sample.

Peer assessment has another almost immeasurable value, too. That is, by assessing others' work, your own improves. Just as research has shown that one of the best ways to learn something is to teach it, the same value comes from assessing others' work. Though we know this to be true, few actually use this technique in the classroom. Many professors have students correct the objective tests of others, but this is not what I'm recommending.

The peer assessment method is so powerful that you'll wonder why you never tried it before. It is a natural outgrowth of the concept of continuous improvement, and based on the measurable operational definitions, gives students real guidelines for assessing without making personal attacks. This also teaches students the value of accepting constructive criticism gracefully. In a real sense, the students are not criticizing, they are assessing each other's work for quality.

By the time the student is ready to turn the product of any learning experience in for assessment by the professor, there should be almost no doubt about whether it is quality. Indeed, the professor is in the position of asking the student if s/he has met all the quality factors. If the answer is YES, then the product is accepted. If the answer is NO, then the student can ask the professor for an assessment and recommendations for improvement. Students then go back and continue working until all quality factors are met. In a quality classroom, the only acceptable product is QUALITY!

DRIVE OUT FEAR
Of course, you'll need to find a way to take the fear out of all this by reducing the dependency on grading. Students must be weaned away from passivity in their learning and become much more proactive. Passivity comes from fear! Educators have succeeded in training students not to evaluate their work, but to create products solely for the professor and to become totally dependent on

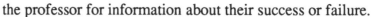

FEAR!

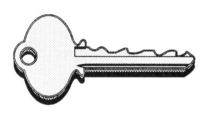

the professor for information about their success or failure.

Clearly, the result of a fear-driven class is not only devastating to the success of the whole, but also to the achievement level of students. Professors who operate in a fear-based culture wonder why students are not motivated.

It is important to reduce fear as much as possible to optimize the learning experience. Some professors fear that anarchy will ensue if they enlist the student's help in resolving classroom process problems. Nothing could be farther from the truth, provided that students believe trust and respect your power within the classroom. Of course, without trust and respect, you'll never be able to come close to a quality classroom, so those issues must be addressed early.

The question of how to coexist within a system that forces you to give grades and have students become comfortable with self-assessment and peer assessment remains. There is really no good answer to that question, probably because as long as grades are involved there will always be a lingering element of fear. But some things can help.

For one thing, for each learning experience it is essential that a time line be established so that everyone can understand the logical cycle time for completion. Within that time line, make it clear to students that they are free to have peer evaluations at any time along the way, as often as they'd like. Encourage students to assess themselves along the way, too. Reduce the dependency on you, to the extent possible, by letting students know that you will be available for guidance and mentoring, but that it is important for them to engage their peers as well. Peer assessments help everyone since the assessor learns as much as the one being assessed. Therefore, assessments are a valuable part of the learning process.

Describe your student evaluation system as presently conducted.

List the steps you are going to take to encourage students to assess their own work and the work of their peers.

How are you going to "Drive Out Fear" in the assessment process?

THE PROFESSOR'S ROLE

A major role of the professor is to be aware of which students are "stuck" and need guidance. This means the professor maintains an active role in facilitating and mentoring. Professors within a quality classroom rarely have time to sit idly while their students are working. Certainly if a general trend becomes apparent, the professor will grab the opportunity to work with a group of students and/or the entire class in clarifying a point or providing further guidance. Perhaps it is a common, frequent grammatical error that students are making. The professor might rightly assume that when this was taught, these students did not learn it well enough to apply it to other situations. In such a case, the professor would be wise to provide students with several examples of proper usage. There should be no shame or blame here, but quality professors will take note, and at a later date do some investigating to determine where the breakdown in learning occurred. Although I will not discuss this in detail, I recommend that when students repeatedly show deficiencies from previous classes that the professor take any such information and recommend a cross-functional team of professors to work together to improve the process at the point of breakdown in order to build quality into the students' education. Since this might become a sensitive point for some professors, it is important to find a way to present the information without shaming or blaming your supplier, *i.e.,* the previous instructor.

PEER TUTORS

Another example of students working with other students is peer tutoring. I really like the idea of having students help others. It provides a very strong, positive experience for all students, especially those who are having difficulty understanding.

Another advantage of using peer tutors is that many times students respond better to their peers, or in one-on-one situations. A rapport can be developed that will pay dividends well beyond one assignment. Once again, it is crucial that all students are trained in some basic principles of peer tutoring. Key among them is to ensure that no one uses coercion or other abusive tactics. Another is that the student being tutored must do the work and not the tutor. Sometimes students become impatient and want to do the work for their friend. In such cases, the one being tutored does not really make many learning gains.

You've probably already guessed that before engaging in any peer tutoring activities, you'll want to gather the class around and generate a discussion about how to optimize the effectiveness of the tutors. Ask students for suggestions about what is most helpful to them and be certain to include some things like being friendly, calm, soft-spoken, etc.

Another very effective technique when you have both older students and

younger students in your class is to have older students buddy up to tutor younger students. This works well on two fronts: (1) it makes the older student feel important and useful, and (2) it gives the younger student a support system beyond the class. Often a rapport develops that extends beyond the classroom into the lunchroom and beyond. Thus young students develop bonds with older students. This technique often makes everyone within the class feel that they share a common goal or purpose. This is truly a unifying force.

CLASSROOM TEAMS

Teams within the classroom can take several forms. There are probably unlimited numbers and purposes of teams within the classroom. I will elaborate on several.

A **Quality Improvement Team** (QIT) functions to collect suggestions for improvement from other students, professors, parents, and administration. This group might be selected randomly and changed every three weeks. There are other ways to select this group, but give everyone in the class an opportunity sometime throughout the semester. It's important not even to hint that only "certain" students will be selected. Invest everyone right away in the realization that this is their classroom and each person has an important role to play. As the names are selected, post them in a prominent place along with the period of time to be served. Next time, be certain not to include any names that were selected during the first round, and so forth until everyone (or almost everyone in large classes) has had a turn.

The importance of this team is to maintain the suggestion box, and/or to collect suggestions from students or teams throughout the semester. These are read with the professor, and a determination is made how to proceed. Encourage students to make suggestions for improvement and post the names of students whose suggestions are implemented.

The team can select a leader who reads to the class any suggested improvement recommendations. Students are then polled to prioritize which suggested improvements they want to implement.

A Quality Leadership Team (QLT) provides over-all leadership to the class. Students are randomly selected from the entire class. The team probably functions best with only three or four members. They, too, should rotate monthly so several groups in the class have the opportunity to participate. They collect data and use quality improvement tools to post the information so everyone can see where improvement takes place and where efforts for improvement still need to be looked at. The QLT works in tandem with the quality improvement team, and often bring ideas forth based on the data they've collected.

The team members work together to determine who will take responsibility for specific duties, what type of data needs to be collected, what form it will take, where it will be posted, and when and how they will report to the class.

What actions are you going to take to establish a **Quality Improvement Team** and a **Quality Leadership Team** in your classes?

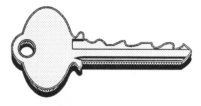

What type of training do you plan to give to the team members? When and how are you going to provide the training?

△△△△△△△△

The following is a checksheet tool to help the professor to implement the **Quality Fusion** technique into the classroom.

Step 1:   The mission, goals, and academic integrity of your course are absolutely clear.

√   Established a course mission statement.
√   Developed personal goals for the course.
√   Communicated mission and goals to the students.
√   Aligned course mission and goals with those of the department (program/major).

Step 2:   You are demonstrating leadership.
√   Developed a definition of a total quality classroom.
√   Walk-the-Talk about quality.
√   Understand Deming's system of **Profound Knowledge**.
√   Use a variety of teaching styles.
√   Have a CQI program for self and for students.

Step 3:   All work is pertinent and flows from the students.
√   Broke down barriers on day one by establishing a course mission statement with the students.
√   Had students co-create learning experiences.
√   Stressed the importance of teamwork in problem solving and decision making.
√   Defined quality and what it means.
√   Created interdisciplinary learning activities.

Step 4:   The course content is connected to the surrounding community and the real world.
√   Demonstrated the connectedness between work and the real world.
√   Asked the students to analyze the learning assignments.
√   Began TQM training for the students.
√   Implemented student suggestions on how best to improve the learning system.

Step 5:   The student is treated as a "worker," but s/he is also considered a valuable team member of the "research and development" department.
√   Gave the students an historical overview about the quality movement and discussed examples.
√   Discussed the P-D-C-A cycle and root causes of problems.

Step 6:   Peer teaching, small group work, and team work are emphasized.
   √   Engaged the students in activities that emphasized teaming and making learning fun.
   √   Engaged students to work independently away from the team, but encouraged them to report the results to their peers.
   √   Provided guidelines and opportunities for students to assess each others' work.
   √   Emphasized the systems approach and regularly asked the students how we could reduce fear.
   √   Provided students with the opportunity for peer tutoring.

Chapter Seven: Students should have aesthetic experiences.

It is possible that students can continue to crank out products for learning experiences that do not involve any creativity on their part, but it is impossible to imagine that anyone would take great joy or pride in doing so. Part of what drives human beings is the desire to create new things—new knowledge as well as new ways of doing something. Thus, creativity can be built into every learning experience simply by asking students how they want to learn. Left to their own devices (with some guidance from professors) students will become more creative, take more learning risks, and value the experience more.

All passes. Art alone
Enduring stays to us.
The Bust outlasts the throne—
The coin, Tiberius.
                    Austin Dobson

Creativity is what has made America great and what has kept us economically ahead of other countries. Creativity is what scientists, inventors, dancers, musicians, and yes, even corporate executives begin with. Asking "what if" leads to our greatest breakthrough inventions, technology, the arts, and even athletics. Everything great starts with an idea. If it can be imagined, it can happen! The axiom is simple, yet very profound.

Part of what makes learning fun is being able to use your creativity and ponder such questions as: what would the world be like without any prejudice...or what will travel be like in the year 2020? These and similar questions force our brains to reach outside our current paradigms and build our current knowledge to create new knowledge. Speculation is one of the first steps to discovery.

Students who have regular opportunities to practice using their imaginations continue to use these skills and eventually become better communicators and more critical thinkers. These skills must be nurtured and allowed to grow, never stifled.

AESTHETICS IN YOUR COURSE

An educated person displays a keen interest in a wide variety of topics and has an appreciation for art, music, theater, and nature. Traditional courses don't do a very good job of nurturing students holistically, yet there is much more to life than the cognitive activities of courses. Quality classrooms are able to engage students in a broad range of activities and demonstrate how they interface with each other.

The systems approach to learning emphasizes that nothing exists by itself, separate from everything else, but that everything is a part of a larger whole. We must provide many opportunities for students to understand the connectedness of their world and the universe to what we are teaching. This presupposes that we have spent time exploring the world beyond our subject matter as well.

What if you created a learning experience that encompassed one or more

of the great artists with music of the period, history, psychology, and great authors of the period; and then study the like from a contemporary perspective? What lessons could be learned from doing that? What if your students did some research on contemporary music and the influence of history and culture on it? What might once have been viewed as a "drag" by students who had to sit through art history or music history classes, could turn into an exciting experience and might forever alter the students' appreciation for the arts. (One of the most interesting courses I taught was "The History of Medicine, Art, and Literature." It was team taught with a professor of art and a professor of literature. Not only were the students interested in looking at the advances in these disciplines, but I also learned a great deal by participating in the course.)

Reflect for a moment on the life most of your students live and the families that they came from. A disproportionate number come from families that have never read a classic novel or heard a symphony. For many of your students, a good family experience is to go home after work and "throw" some burgers on the grill and have a beer or two. Then for relaxation, several hours in front of the TV before the going to bed. The next day the cycle starts over again. Many never really appreciate the mountains, a natural lake, streams, or the forests. Imagine, they are living a life without appreciating either natural beauty, or having witnessed the spiritual beauty of the Redwood forest or some of our spectacular national parks. Imagine never seeing the beauty of the Grand Canyon, the lush green Appalachian Trail, the stark beauty of the desert, the intriguing swamps of Louisiana and Florida or the vast expanse of the Great Lakes. Too many of your students have never experienced many of these things.

Last, I contend that students and professors today live with far too many stresses and not many opportunities to relieve them so they can be free to learn, let alone experience joy in learning. Therefore, I suggest the use of reflection time for students to relax and practice deep breathing at the start of every class. Even Covey (1989) recognized the importance of self-renewal: his seventh habit is to "Sharpen the Saw."

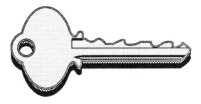

What specific actions are you going to implement within the next 45 days to help you and your students reflect on creative activities?

What specific actions are you going to implement within the next 45 days to help you and your students to grow and develop more of an appreciation for art, music, theater, nature, and world events?

What specific actions are you going to implement within the next 45 days to help you and your students to establish a healthier life style?

What specific data are you going to gather to evaluate and improve on the actions taken?

△△△△△△△△

The following is a checksheet tool to help the professor to implement the **Quality Fusion** technique into the classroom.

Step 1: The mission, goals, and academic integrity of your course are absolutely clear.
  √ Established a course mission statement.
  √ Developed personal goals for the course.
  √ Communicated mission and goals to the students.
  √ Aligned course mission and goals with those of the department (program/major).

Step 2: You are demonstrating leadership.
  √ Developed a definition of a total quality classroom.
  √ Walk-the-Talk about quality.
  √ Understand Deming's system of **Profound Knowledge**.
  √ Use a variety of teaching styles.
  √ Have a CQI program for self and for students.

Step 3: All work is pertinent and flows from the students.
  √ Broke down barriers on day one by establishing a course mission statement with the students.
  √ Had students co-create learning experiences.
  √ Stressed the importance of teamwork in problem solving and decision making.
  √ Defined quality and what it means.
  √ Created interdisciplinary learning activities.

Step 4: The course content is connected to the surrounding community and the real world.
  √ Demonstrated the connectedness between work and the real world.
  √ Asked the students to analyze the learning assignments.
  √ Began TQM training for the students.
  √ Implemented student suggestions on how best to improve the learning system.

Step 5: The student is treated as a "worker," but s/he is also considered a valuable team member of the "research and development" department.
  √ Gave the students an historical overview about the quality movement and discussed examples.
  √ Discussed the P-D-C-A cycle and root causes of problems.

Step 6: Peer teaching, small group work, and team work are emphasized.
√ Engaged the students in activities that emphasized teaming and making learning fun.
√ Engaged students to work independently away from the team, but encouraged them to report the results to their peers.
√ Provided guidelines and opportunities for students to assess each others' work.
√ Emphasized the systems approach and regularly asked the students how we could reduce fear.
√ Provided students with the opportunity for peer tutoring.
√ Elaborated upon the types of quality teams.
√ Introduced the students to additional TQI tools and techniques.

Step 7: Students should have aesthetic experiences.
√ Encouraged students to use their imagination daily.
√ Discussed the importance of art, music, nature, relaxation techniques, meditation, diet, and exercise with one or more of my students.
√ Discussed news headlines and/or controversial topics with one or more of the students.
√ Gathered specific data to evaluate and improve creative experiences.

Chapter Eight: Classroom processes should include reflection.

Seldom within the educational setting do either professors or students have time to reflect on their work or their goals or their accomplishments. We seem to focus on the "doing" of things rather than "why" we are doing them. Often professors will say they have no time to think; no time to pause and reflect on the teaching/learning process or about the progress the class or individuals are making. Yet without adequate reflection time, things seem to go on and on and never get any better.

We must give serious thought to the necessity for reflection. In the Plan—Do—Study—Act (PDSA) cycle, the planning phase is crucial—see Figure 8.1. It is the phase that provides the foundations for every process, and includes reflection on cause and effect as well as study of current processes for "best practice." **Without adequate reflection and planning it is simply not possible to build quality into the processes that make up the activity of the classroom.**

Figure 8.1 P-D-S-A Cycle

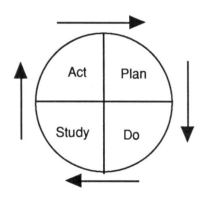

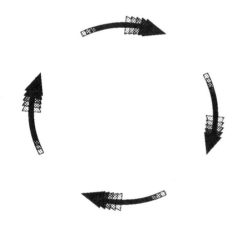

Most professors spend 50 to 60 hours a week doing work for their institution. They are constantly preparing and/or revising lectures, reading about the advances in their area of specialization, writing grant proposals, doing research, advising students, participating on department, school, and institutional committees. Some are actively involved in providing services for their community and/or their national organization. They attend meetings in order to keep themselves professionally developed.

Most professors would probably agree that they take little or no time to reflect on their mission and goals and performance in the classroom. Most would probably agree that some processes are not working optimally, and that if they obtained help from students and/or colleagues, the learning environment as well as learning experiences could be improved.

INSTANT FEEDBACK

In a quality classroom professors should engage the students to help them reflect on various classroom processes each day. This might be called fast feedback, or debriefing, or simply reflection time. The essence of this is that professors cannot possibly carry the burden for learning. Shared responsibility and shared decision making is one of the tenets of quality. For example, a fast feedback form for a computer class might look like this:

Table 8.1: Fast Feedback Form

Activity	Too Fast	—	OK	—	Too Slow
Data Base	5	4	3	2	1
Word Processing	5	4	3	2	1
Spreadsheet	5	4	3	2	1

Almost instantly the professor will recognize who needs help and which student(s) would benefit from some peer assistance.

Next day the professor could reorganize the class into groups with at least one student who was excelling at the particular activity and one who was having some difficulty. In this way, students could help each other and the professor could be of greater help to the entire class by moving between groups.

She might also ask the students for more general information about what they need to make the activities more interesting or to help them learn.

Professors of mathematics in our colleges and universities might borrow a lesson from what the Japanese elementary teachers do. In their elementary schools, one concept (one problem) is presented each day and it is always a real world problem. Students work in teams to resolve the problem. The teacher prepares the problem and provides each team with a copy, then writes the problem on the board. Then, she reads the problem to the entire class. Students first attempt to solve the problem on their own, writing down the steps in their logic journal. Next, the team discusses the problem and members compare their notes. For second graders this will be rudimentary, but if college students get into the habit of writing their thinking down, they more readily learn the logic errors they've made and can self-correct many of them.

The teacher's role is to present the problem and then allow students time to reflect on the answer. Towards the end of the time, the teacher brings the class together for a discussion of the problem by asking teams what answer they came up with. She never indicates right or wrong, but moves from one team to the next until all have given their answer.

Next, she calls on the team who has gotten the problem wrong to look at their logic journals and tell the group how they arrived at the answer. Throughout the process, no one shouts out the answer, but the teacher carefully guides them through the process. Generally, as students discuss the logic of their answers they quickly pick up where they made a mistake and will say something like, "Oh, I see that can't possibly be correct." The teacher encourages the team to go back, review their logic journals and see what they come up with. All the time, the teacher must resist giving the correct answer or allowing others to shout out the answer. If necessary, s/he may have one or more teams work together, perhaps one which got the correct answer paired with another that did not. Using this method, assuming that all the students fully understand the concept that the problem was meant to get across, there is no need for homework.

College professors could employ the same method as the Japanese do in their elementary school mathematics classes. In fact, all math problems should be application problems with real world models or examples.

A fast feedback form for a statistics class might look like:

Table 8.2: Fast Feedback Form For Statistics

Circle the number that best represents your thoughts on today's work.

1 = Strongly Agree   2 = Agree
3 = Somewhat Disagree   4 = Disagree

1. I understand the logic of today's problem.
        1   2   3   4
2. I could apply this logic to another situation.
        1   2   3   4
3. This class is moving at a good pace for me.
        1   2   3   4

Signature (optional):

Professors would do well to allow their students to give them continuous feedback much like that suggested above. Unless we know (specifically and systematically) what difficulties the students encounter, how can we possibly know how to create a better learning environment or learning experience? (The examples above are not meant to be the only feedback questions that are valid or useful.) The professor probably would want to experiment with these and with practice discover how to ask questions that provide the best information in a short amount of time.

I recommend that students be given the option of signing their names so that the professor can provide them with the help needed. If a third or more of the students report that the class is moving too slow or too fast, the professor would be wise to find a way to accommodate them. The optimum use of time is to have most of the students (with just a few reporting too fast or too slow) reporting that they agree, or number 2. After the students get accustomed to fast feedback, you can random sample students rather than the entire class.

Never underestimate the power of students' help. They reflect on classes often outside of school and/or during class when you may surmise they are daydreaming. They are the ones working in the system and, therefore, are in the best position to offer assistance about ways to build quality into the system or process.

STUDENT REFLECTION

Another valuable resource for students is reflection. Rarely do we provide opportunities for students to participate in any reflection about their work or the work of their team or classmates. By not doing so, in essence educators perpetuate the short term recall and pay little attention to the larger questions that arise with learning experiences that require students to do research and create new knowledge. Whenever one is engaged in creating new knowledge or testing a new theory, reflection is a critical step.

Human thought is like a monstrous pendulum: It keeps swinging from one extreme to the other.
Eugene Field

Students who engage in regular reflective time also seem to gain insights into their own lives and behaviors in the context of the larger world. This leads to goal setting and valuable lifelong skills. This self-assessment requires each student to reflect on her/his behavior and performance for the week and to set personal goals. The results from this type of activity have kept the students more focused, thus allowing them to learn more each week. Students like the idea of having to write personal goals and engage in some reflection and self-assessment. In fact, some students report they have their families and friends engage in goal setting.

Students can engage in **Force Field Analysis** and other continuous improvement tools that cause them to reflect on behavior and habits leading to success or failure. You might want to include regular times for your students to complete a force field analysis on their efforts to improve the overall quality of the class. Or this could become part of a total class effort led by the quality leadership team, and students could engage in cause/effect diagrams also.

The method or continuous quality improvement tool you select is not nearly as important as taking the time to include reflection as a routine part of the quality classroom. Students and professors both can benefit from this activity. I suggest that students fill a notebook with the story of their continuous quality improvement journey. Such a notebook can be filled with pages of force field analyses, cause/effect diagrams, etc. This can become part of their portfolio and is evidence to them as well as their parents and professors that they've grown in their reflective ability and improved their performance as a result.

ΔΔΔΔΔΔΔΔΔ

The following is a checksheet tool to help the professor to implement the **Quality Fusion** technique into the classroom.

Step 1: The mission, goals, and academic integrity of your course are absolutely clear.
  √ Established a course mission statement.
  √ Developed personal goals for the course.
  √ Communicated mission and goals to the students.
  √ Aligned course mission and goals with those of the department (program/major).

Step 2: You are demonstrating leadership.
  √ Developed a definition of a total quality classroom.
  √ Walk-the-Talk about quality.
  √ Understand Deming's system of **Profound Knowledge**.
  √ Use a variety of teaching styles.
  √ Have a CQI program for self and for students.

Step 3: All work is pertinent and flows from the students.
  √ Broke down barriers on day one by establishing a course mission statement with the students.
  √ Had students co-create learning experiences.
  √ Stressed the importance of teamwork in problem solving and decision making.
  √ Defined quality and what it means.
  √ Created interdisciplinary learning activities.

Step 4: The course content is connected to the surrounding community and the real world.

√ Demonstrated the connectedness between work and the real world.

√ Asked the students to analyze the learning assignments.

√ Began TQM training for the students.

√ Implemented student suggestions on how best to improve the learning system.

Step 5: The student is treated as a "worker," but s/he is also considered a valuable team member of the "research and development" department.

√ Gave the students an historical overview about the quality movement and discussed examples.

√ Discussed the P-D-C-A cycle and root causes of problems.

Step 6: Peer teaching, small group work, and team work are emphasized.

√ Engaged the students in activities that emphasized teaming and making learning fun.

√ Engaged students to work independently away from the team, but encouraged them to report the results to their peers.

√ Provided guidelines and opportunities for students to assess each others' work.

√ Emphasized the systems approach and regularly asked the students how we could reduce fear.

√ Provided students with the opportunity for peer tutoring.

√ Elaborated upon the types of quality teams.

√ Introduced the students to additional TQI tools and techniques.

Step 7: Students should have aesthetic experiences.

√ Encouraged students to use their imagination daily.

√ Discussed the importance of art, music, nature, relaxation techniques, meditation, diet, and exercise with one or more of my students.

√ Discussed news headlines and/or controversial topics with one or more of the students.

√ Gathered specific data to evaluate and improve creative experiences.

Step 8: Classroom processes include reflection.
√ Developed instant feedback form with students in order to measure classroom processes.
√ Distributed instant feedback forms in order to examine classroom processes.
√ Reflected on my mission, goals, and classroom processes.
√ Set time aside for students to reflect on the relevance of course work to real world issues and encouraged them to discuss their perceptions.
√ Developed self-assessment and goal-setting instruments with students.

Chapter Nine: The teaching/learning system should undergo constant evaluation.

It is very important that the teaching/learning process continuously be assessed. This can be accomplished daily and/or weekly through a variety of methods. It is critical to the continuous quality improvement of the class, and its importance must not be overlooked. In fact, without it, your course is not likely to improve as quickly, if at all. Unfortunately, some professors are frightened by the possibility of having their work under such close scrutiny. They have become used to doing all the planning, creating, and teaching with only the scrutiny of the department chairperson (or peer review team) several times per year if their name falls into the evaluation cycle for that year. This has suited many professors just right except when the reviewer makes some suggestions for improvement. Then too many professors become defensive and view the review as punishment rather than an opportunity for positive growth.

Just like students, professors become upset when they feel they've been rated and are not at the top. Professors have difficulty understanding how they can give up the A-F grading scale when that seems fair to them (because they are not the ones being rated), yet they cannot translate their feelings about evaluation to the students. What an interesting dichotomy—one that deserves more time than this work allows. However, I hope to make the paradigm shift away from a once or twice each year external evaluation system to the hope and encouragement that can be found in regular, routine assessment from students and the professor him/herself.

Many quality experts agree that ratings and yearly evaluations for raises or merit pay are destructive to the organization as they decrease morale and sense of stature. Individuals who are made to feel as if they are contributing less without any help from the system to improve their performance are likely to have lower self-esteem, produce less, and be angry.

Professors need to understand how destructive their attitudes about assessment of self and students are. The first premise that we must agree on is that no one is perfect. If you agree with that, then you can probably also agree that improvement is much faster when the environment is free of fear and fosters growth and continuous feedback.

Fear is really at the heart of the problem. Some deans and department chairpersons want/need everyone to like them. These are the people who don't like the process of having to do classroom visitations for the purpose of evaluating the professor and become uncomfortable with the idea that they may say something to hurt the professor's feelings. Such an administrator may rate every professor the same—either excellent in all categories, or above average in all categories. It is doubtful that an administrator with this type personality would rate all professors "average." The professors naturally talk amongst themselves after the administrator leaves. If it appears that everyone gets the same rating then all is well, though the dean/department chairperson may be subjected to some criticism once the professors leave the building and get home. They will invariably make comments somewhat like this, "I don't understand how Bob could have gotten the same rating as I got, when everyone knows all he does is give all of his students A's."

Administrators like those described above are not helpful. In their zeal to make everyone appear to have the same competencies, they do not help their professors, and isn't that the purpose of the evaluation? In traditional colleges, the dean is the educational leader of the school. Good leaders allow people to take risks, to make mistakes and then learn from them, and encourage those who are struggling by helping provide what they need to improve.

On the other hand, when a dedicated dean goes into the classroom and takes notes and fills out a check sheet it makes many professors nervous. Some even become hostile that s/he dares to make any judgments based on one or two observations. In essence we have created a monster when it comes to assessing professor performance. It has, in many colleges, become a hotly contested negotiating point, and has resulted in less than desired results no matter what format the assessment takes.

In a passing note: in the fourteen state universities in the State System for Higher Education in Pennsylvania, a dean cannot enter the classroom to evaluate a professor. S/he has to make the evaluation based on written documentation. How the chancellor's office permitted this to happen is beyond sound logic and good management principles.

In colleges and universities, peers evaluate each other. This makes professors nervous because they wonder who made the select few "God," and leads to isolation for those chosen to be the evaluators. Of course, one cannot generalize these responses to include the universe, but suffice it to say the negative aspects of professor evaluations far outweigh the good that might come from engaging in **continuous assessment**.

An important part of the idea of assessment is that everyone can improve and no one is ever "there." Indeed, "there" in a quality classroom continues to move forward, making stretch goals the norm for everyone including professors and students.

PROFESSOR ASSESSMENT
In terms of professor assessment, I recommend two things. First, professors engage in a yearly self-assessment based on the Malcolm Baldrige Award Criteria as described in *The Quality Professor: Implementing TQM in the Classroom* (1993). It examines seven categories to measure the quality of the classroom system, namely:

1. Leadership
2. Information and Analysis
3. Strategic Quality Planning
4. Human Resource Utilization
5. Quality Assurance of Products and Services
6. Quality Results
7. Customer Satisfaction

This takes the assessment process out of the subjective (anecdotes are not sufficient to describe trends, achievement, and improvement) and into the objective. Once the self-assessment instrument is completed, the professor is asked to prepare an action plan based on the department's identified priority goals. Upon meeting with the dean or Quality Council, each professor is then offered the help s/he needs to make the desired improvements.

Second, professors are curious about the TQM concept that students, as "workers" within the system, are in the best position to help improve it and build quality into each process in the beginning. Professors must come to recognize that they cannot get along without regular feedback from their students. Once you try this, and can let go of any sense of defensiveness or personal attack, you will discover the merits of allowing students to help.

I suggest that you examine your fears in relation to having students help assess the teaching/learning process. Perhaps you fear that if given a chance, anarchy will ensue. To this, I ask that you recall a time when you were having a difficult time in a given class. Perhaps you were bored. Perhaps the subject matter was confusing. Maybe the professor was moving too quickly or too slowly and the assignments were meaningless. Whatever the situation, the question is, if that professor had asked you for input could/would you have been willing to help? The answer is probably, YES! Why then, do you fear anarchy when you take the risk and ask students? They will be only too happy to help. Besides a willingness to help, the students will feel empowered and have more ownership of the class.

A word of caution: if you ask students for help in assessing the teaching/learning process then you have to be ready for whatever they say and listen without judgment. The minute you become defensive or try to explain, they will realize that you aren't really serious. If that happens you will have some problems with the students because you'll have broken the trust bond between you and it will take a long time to repair. Sometimes when we "create" something, our sense of ownership is so great that any criticism or suggestion is taken negatively. You can think about this in a more detached way if you can remember your constancy of purpose. The purpose of any professor should be to optimize the students' learning. College isn't about teaching, it is about learning!

I strongly urge you to reach out to your students. Explain to them what

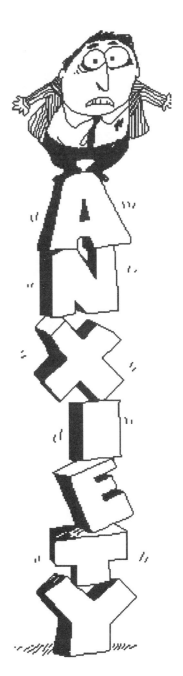

you're doing and the necessity you see in doing it. Unless every one of your students is currently operating at 100 percent efficiency, there is room for improvement.

DEBRIEFING

Debriefing can take many forms. It is always important to do some type of debriefing after every learning experience, especially if your goal is continuous improvement. It takes just a minute or two but can yield very powerful and invaluable information for professors. Student members of your quality leadership team can assist with the tabulation efforts. That process might take them 10 minutes for a class of 30 students. As they become more familiar with the debriefing sheet, the time to tabulate the responses will become less. It certainly is more powerful to have students do as much of this as possible, but if it is too frightening for you, then you can tabulate it yourself. Either way, in a very short time you've gotten feedback that you can use to alter the resources, materials, and lecture you used.

Be prepared to consider what, if anything, you'll do if one-fourth or one-third of all students say your lectures were no help at all? I recommend you drop whatever sense of ownership you feel about those carefully prepared lectures and let go of them, or at a minimum modify them and continue to ask for feedback on their usefulness. Sometimes too much of ourselves is wrapped up in what we do, and for professors, often that is lecture. Remember the purpose: optimize the students' learning. If the lectures are not helpful, then let them go and be relieved that your students have felt they could be honest with you. It only hurts the first time, believe me.

Other debriefing efforts can be in the form of fast feedback which is used daily to assess how students felt they progressed that day in completing the learning experience. Fast feedback approaches depend on the class and the type of students. Structure your questions to solicit responses that will prove the most helpful for the following day. Some professors prefer to use a very open-ended approach, others prefer the Likert Scale, and others a Yes/No response. Questions using the Likert Scale can be especially enlightening if they are worded correctly; otherwise, you may not get the kind of information you need.

Whenever you use fast feedback, start by asking yourself what you need to know in order to improve the teaching/learning process for all the students. You don't need to know the names of all respondents, but it certainly would help you provide some assistance to students who indicate they need help. If anonymity is important to the students, then it would be wise to comply with their wishes. I recommend that you leave signature optional and stress that if students are having difficulty then you can best help if you know what their specific needs are.

Like most things having to do with quality, honest answers are predicated on trust. It takes a tremendous amount of trust for students to feel totally free to respond honestly rather than with what they think will please the professor. Too often in colleges, professors withhold respect from students who are honest with them. As Calvin from *Calvin & Hobbs* says, "It isn't fair to kill the messenger." When you ask for feedback, be willing to listen and remember the **purpose** for asking: **to improve the teaching/learning system.** The most effective professors are those who seek and use suggestions from students since doing so enhances trust, pride, cooperation, and teamwork.

Knowledge comes, but wisdom lingers.
Tennyson

STUDENT DEBRIEFING

As with professors, students need to debrief as well. The format should be determined based on the type of learning experience the students just completed. Debriefing may start as an individual or team effort and then progress to the class as a whole. It may be formal, as in having students complete a questionnaire, or informal by having discussion follow some sort of format. In either case, results should be recorded and analyzed for making decisions about future projects, learning experiences, team selection, materials, etc.

With informal debriefings, I recommend a student be selected (providing leadership opportunities to all students) to lead the discussion. Typical interview questions that a student quality improvement representative might ask of the class.

- The thing I liked best about this learning experience was:

- The thing that I didn't like was:

- The best thing about my group was:

- The thing I'd like to change about my group was:

- These kinds of learning experiences are:

- The thing(s) I learned from this is/are:

Have a student write all responses on the board and then create a **Pareto Chart** to determine the most critical problem(s). This information can be used to set parameters for the next learning experience.

The Pareto Diagram identifies the few significant factors that contribute to a problem and separates them from the significant factors.

PORTFOLIO AND SELF-ASSESSMENT
As your course moves more toward quality, teach the students to perform regular self-assessments. This is usually something new for the students, and you'll need to teach your students some ways to do it. One of the first things you'll want to do is post the quality factors and operational definitions and also be certain each student has a copy for each learning experience. These provide the guideposts for students as they determine whether or not they've achieved quality. Everything that is done in the classroom should be under the guise of the quality factors and **operational definitions**.

ΔΔΔΔΔΔΔΔ

The following is a checksheet tool to help the professor to implement the **Quality Fusion** technique into the classroom.

Step 1: The mission, goals, and academic integrity of your course are absolutely clear.
    √ Established a course mission statement.
    √ Developed personal goals for the course.
    √ Communicated mission and goals to the students.
    √ Aligned course mission and goals with those of the department (program/major).

Step 2: You are demonstrating leadership.
    √ Developed a definition of a total quality classroom.
    √ Walk-the-Talk about quality.
    √ Understand Deming's system of **Profound Knowledge**.
    √ Use a variety of teaching styles.
    √ Have a CQI program for self and for students.

Step 3: All work is pertinent and flows from the students.
    √ Broke down barriers on day one by establishing a course mission statement with the students.
    √ Had students co-create learning experiences.
    √ Stressed the importance of teamwork in problem solving and decision making.
    √ Defined quality and what it means.
    √ Created interdisciplinary learning activities.

Step 4:   The course content is connected to the surrounding community and the real world.
√ Demonstrated the connectedness between work and the real world.
√ Asked the students to analyze the learning assignments.
√ Began TQM training for the students.
√ Implemented student suggestions on how best to improve the learning system.

Step 5:   The student is treated as a "worker," but s/he is also considered a valuable team member of the "research and development" department.
√ Gave the students an historical overview about the quality movement and discussed examples.
√ Discussed the P-D-C-A cycle and root causes of problems.

Step 6:   Peer teaching, small group work, and team work are emphasized.
√ Engaged the students in activities that emphasized teaming and making learning fun.
√ Engaged students to work independently away from the team, but encouraged them to report the results to their peers.
√ Provided guidelines and opportunities for students to assess each others' work.
√ Emphasized the systems approach and regularly asked the students how we could reduce fear.
√ Provided students with the opportunity for peer tutoring.
√ Elaborated upon the types of quality teams.
√ Introduced the students to additional TQI tools and techniques.

Step 7:   Students should have aesthetic experiences.
√ Encouraged students to use their imagination daily.
√ Discussed the importance of art, music, nature, relaxation techniques, meditation, diet, and exercise with one or more of my students.
√ Discussed news headlines and/or controversial topics with one or more of the students.
√ Gathered specific data to evaluate and improve creative experiences.

Step 8: Classroom processes include reflection.

√ Developed instant feedback form with students in order to measure classroom processes.

√ Distributed instant feedback forms in order to examine classroom processes.

√ Reflected on my mission, goals, and classroom processes.

√ Set time aside for students to reflect on the relevance of course work to real world issues and encouraged them to discuss their perceptions.

√ Developed self-assessment and goal-setting instruments with students.

Step 9: The teaching/learning system is constantly evaluated.

√ Used modified Malcolm Baldrige Quality Award Criteria to judge the effectiveness of my classroom processes.

√ Refined my professional work plan and based it on the mission and goals of my department and school.

√ Discussed my professional work plan with my dean.

√ Constantly interviewed and surveyed my students as to the effectiveness of the teaching/learning system.

√ Taught students additional TQI tools, including the use of portfolios for self-assessment.

Chapter 10:   New activities should constantly evolve from the old.

In quality classrooms there is never an absolute end to learning; rather, learning experiences simply evolve one from another, and the flow of knowledge continues to build with new concepts being introduced in a wave-like fashion. In the traditional model of learning, one concept is introduced with lessons directly related to it, work is assigned, then students take a test to determine their rate of learning. Whether or not the concept was learned, students continue on to the next and the next. The ramifications of this approach to learning are that many students don't understand basic concepts and then are forever behind those who do. There are no provisions to ensure all students gain the necessary knowledge to move on. Hence, there are failures and in some cases, students are being held back.

I propose a very different approach to learning. In this model students start with the competencies they are expected to achieve during any semester. This list of competencies is determined by the professor, not by students.

The competencies must be continuously reviewed and upgraded as students learn more and achieve more using the quality learning approach. This means that even though the outcomes may be listed, they must be fluid enough so that students who go beyond what is expected are not penalized or put into a "holding" pattern, but can continue to move forward.

Robert Gavin, the CEO of Motorola, recently suggested to a group of educators that they start thinking about how they can pack fifty percent more into each class they teach. He said that this was the kind of thinking that Motorola had to do in order to be competitive and stay in business. Furthermore, this continues to be the challenge of business—to do more in less time with less money and to continue to improve the product to satisfy customers while anticipating their future needs.

Many educators do not feel the sense of urgency of business because of the belief that higher education will always remain a mainstay in America. The tragedy of this kind of thinking is that there is no real understanding of how the work of higher education (as a system) interacts with business or the systems that comprise our communities. It seems that professors would benefit from summer internships in TQM operated businesses wherein they would shadow the employees from the corporate leader to those on the factory floor. The principle of continuous improvement is a way of life in companies that expect to stay in business. For those who ignore the customer, their suppliers, and their competition, success (if there is any) will be fleeting and those companies will soon be out of business. It is a fact that we *must* change the way we do business in higher education: **we can no longer sit back and pretend that we are doing a good job or that our students are competitive in the global economy**.

For confidence is the son of vision, and is sired by information.

Cornelius Vanderbilt, Jr.

ACCEPTING THE STUDENT AS CUSTOMER AND WORKER

You should accept the idea that students are both your primary customer and also the workers within the system. As such, they are in the best position (as previously stated) to help make suggestions for improving the system to build in quality. Next, recognize that everything that is done in the classroom must be student focused, and nothing should interfere with that constancy of purpose: to optimize the learning experiences for all students.

EXPANDING THE VISION

Professors, students, and parents have all been brainwashed into believing that only a certain amount of material can be learned within the academic year. The problem with this limiting belief is that students learn even less because professors can't imagine how to get through the book anyway.

Some educators would have us believe that society sends us defective kids, and without those kids and all their problems, professors would have time to teach more and students would achieve more. That is an interesting argument, but one that doesn't hold up under scrutiny. It is akin to the argument that if more money were put into the educational system then professors could do a better job and students would learn more. Neither of these makes any real sense, but are and have been convenient excuses that many use and too many others believe.

By the same token, the purpose of college is not to house professors or to employ professors, but to optimize the learning experiences of students. Colleges are about learning—not teaching! Yes, you can learn without having a professor, but that is not what I am subscribing to. I use that statement simply to make the point, that learning and teaching are two different and separate events. Just as someone can teach yet no one learn—the same can be said for the reverse; someone can learn yet no one has taught. Remember this, it will be helpful to you in creating a quality classroom.

So, without excuses for the way things are, you must focus on the vision of the future. Create your vision of the optimal learning environment. What does it look like, sound like? What kinds of activities are going on? How are students organized? Create this vision and imagine your utopia in an educational setting. To do this, it will be necessary to eliminate all your biases about people, the community, the college, the world. Eliminate them and open yourself to the possibilities of having *all* your students achieve far beyond your wildest imagination. Include in your vision of excellence those students who have been difficult for you, those with disabilities, and those who are different. This is a learning environment that is totally without fear and where students help each other, where the professor is the leader, mentor, and facilitator and learner right along with the students.

How can you change the vision from the traditional to the new— towards continuous quality learning? I recommend strongly that students be allowed to co-create these learning experiences. Professors can and should start the process by creating the first one or two experiences, but beyond that students can play a major role in determining their own learning experiences.

With students as co-creators of learning experiences, professors need spend little time creating lectures. The course goals and competencies are created together as the semester progresses. If everyone knows what is expected, why do professors have to be rigid in determining how these competencies will be achieved? If students are allowed to help in creating the learning experiences, they will be motivated to accomplish them. In the traditional view, professors are responsible for planning and creating everything that happens in their course. The problem is that either only those students who are eager to please the professors or who are blessed with some internal discipline that keeps them focused will buy into your assignments.

I suggest that even those students one typically thinks of as being fully challenged are only about half challenged and that we have absolutely no idea how far they could advance if given the opportunity to co-create their own learning experiences. The majority who seem unmotivated or disinterested in college will never do any better than they currently do unless something dramatic changes in the system to make a learning environment that works for them. Do not sell these students short. They are NOT unmotivated to learn!

One of the most frequent complaints students have about college is that most course content lacks relevance to the real world. If students don't know how something can benefit them, they most likely will not fully invest in learning it. They might do the "work," but few will retain it other than in their short term memory, and if asked the following year to build on previously learned concepts, they will have no recollection of learning it at all. This is frustrating for professors who have worked so hard only to discover that their students go to the next class where the next instructor complains that the students weren't taught the necessary prerequisites for success in their course.

Imagine taking an entirely different approach to the teaching/learning process. Imagine asking the students how they want to learn the desired outcomes and for input into how much time they need to learn. Imagine creating a **systematic diagram** together that shows specific tasks and the order each should be done, along with a time table and an indication of who's responsible. This is the way to engage students and relieve yourself of the burden of daily lectures. Of course, you'll have to guide this process, but allow the students as much freedom as possible.

The Systematic Diagram is used as a planning tool to determine specific actions that are necessary to accomplish a broader goal.

You must believe that you can assist all students to learn even the most complex concepts in your course, provided you find ways to create an experience that they perceive as fun, interesting, and intriguing, and always related to their world.

When creating a learning experience, do it with the end in mind. What would you like the students to know, demonstrate, or create at the end of this experience? Point out the competencies that are included in this experience. Discuss the ways they will demonstrate they've achieved each of these outcomes. Then, they will know your expectations.

Each day you'll want students to give you a minute of their time for fast feedback. This is the way you'll keep updated on how each student is progressing, where their frustrations are, and how you can help. If you don't have the opportunity to get to each student each day, the fast feedback will give you very valuable information.

Of course, you've set a time limit for this activity, and students have created a **Systematic Diagram** for themselves or a **Flow Chart** with key process points fixed so you can assess how they are doing.

NEW ACTIVITIES FROM THE OLD

When the first learning experience (particular competencies) is over, you should debrief your students so you can get a clear picture of what worked for them and what didn't. Have students review the competencies for the semester and see how they can build upon the previously learned ones. Then brainstorm with students how they want to build onto this experience. Allow everyone time to share their ideas and move towards building consensus. The product they end up with may be very different, but the learning experience can be the same for all.

Imagine your students building upon this first learning experience by wanting to do something to make the college a better place to learn. They might research opportunities in student aide, financial services, admissions, computer center, library, and/or housing, or there may be some pressing concern that interests them. Build a consensus among students as to what direction they would like the learning experience to take and write the purpose (mission) on the board. Next, ask students what they'd consider quality factors. This will be the basis for evaluation or the expectations upon which their projects will be assessed. Next, ask students what they would say if they were to describe the "best" way to accomplish the project. In other words, you will want students to define their expectations. If they don't come up with all the pertinent quality factors, then you, as a partner in the class, can add yours.

Prior to asking students to commence, review the expected terminal course competencies and see which one(s) will be accomplished by completing the learning experience. Have students again go through and circle those that apply, and place a small check mark at the level at which the class agrees each competency must be achieved.

With students create a flow chart of the process that will be used for this learning experience. Students will then have a picture of how the learning experience will unfold and what the process check points will be. You can add a time line and identify the person responsible on any flow chart simply by creating a deployment flow chart and adding dates.

With this method students have information that gives them a clear picture of expectations, responsibilities, check points, and results. Everyone knows what is expected, and everyone knows what criteria will be used to assess the final product. This takes away excuses, but more importantly allows students the freedom to work without fear of a breakdown in the process. Enthusiasm will run high when the learning environment and learning experiences are established collaboratively, with students identifying their products.

THE FINAL PRODUCT

We've been schooled to believe that an assignment means that everyone does the same thing. In quality classrooms there is plenty of room for creativity and invention. Many students may be creating new and different products from the others', though the competency is the same for all. Remember the importance of the constancy of purpose and think about how to optimize the learning experiences for all students. Some students may view the product visually, others will want to write, while still others will want to use a different approach. With time, all students can expand their approach to learning by experiencing it in many forms.

Through a process of teaching students how to create learning experiences that are fun and real-world oriented, and then applying quality improvement tools for planning and studying the results, students can and do become fully engaged in their own learning. These students are enthusiastic and energetic learners, eager to stretch the limits of their knowledge and hence their world.

At the end of each school year students will be eager to sign up for your courses. In classrooms where quality improvement is a way of life, students eagerly work past the last day of school, and will drive you crazy when they continually contact you during your summer sabbatical.

△△△△△△△△△

The following is a checksheet tool to help the professor to implement the **Quality Fusion** technique into the classroom.

Step 1: The mission, goals, and academic integrity of your course are absolutely clear.
√ Established a course mission statement.
√ Developed personal goals for the course.
√ Communicated mission and goals to the students.
√ Aligned course mission and goals with those of the department (program/major).

Step 2: You are demonstrating leadership.
√ Developed a definition of a total quality classroom.
√ Walk-the-Talk about quality.
√ Understand Deming's system of **Profound Knowledge**.
√ Use a variety of teaching styles.
√ Have a CQI program for self and for students.

Step 3: All work is pertinent and flows from the students.
√ Broke down barriers on day one by establishing a course mission statement with the students.
√ Had students co-create learning experiences.
√ Stressed the importance of teamwork in problem solving and decision making.
√ Defined quality and what it means.
√ Created interdisciplinary learning activities.

Step 4: The course content is connected to the surrounding community and the real world.
√ Demonstrated the connectedness between work and the real world.
√ Asked the students to analyze the learning assignments.
√ Began TQM training for the students.
√ Implemented student suggestions on how best to improve the learning system.

Step 5: The student is treated as a "worker," but s/he is also considered a valuable team member of the "research and development" department.
√ Gave the students an historical overview about the quality movement and discussed examples.
√ Discussed the P-D-C-A cycle and root causes of problems.

Step 6: Peer teaching, small group work, and team work are emphasized.

√ Engaged the students in activities that emphasized teaming and making learning fun.

√ Engaged students to work independently away from the team, but encouraged them to report the results to their peers.

√ Provided guidelines and opportunities for students to assess each others' work.

√ Emphasized the systems approach and regularly asked the students how we could reduce fear.

√ Provided students with the opportunity for peer tutoring.

√ Elaborated upon the types of quality teams.

√ Introduced the students to additional TQI tools and techniques.

Step 7: Students should have aesthetic experiences.

√ Encouraged students to use their imagination daily.

√ Discussed the importance of art, music, nature, relaxation techniques, meditation, diet, and exercise with one or more of my students.

√ Discussed news headlines and/or controversial topics with one or more of the students.

√ Gathered specific data to evaluate and improve creative experiences.

Step 8: Classroom processes include reflection.

√ Developed instant feedback form with students in order to measure classroom processes.

√ Distributed instant feedback forms in order to examine classroom processes.

√ Reflected on my mission, goals, and classroom processes.

√ Set time aside for students to reflect on the relevance of course work to real world issues and encouraged them to discuss their perceptions.

√ Developed self-assessment and goal-setting instruments with students.

Step 9:   The teaching/learning system is constantly evaluated.
- √   Used modified Malcolm Baldrige Quality Award Criteria to judge the effectiveness of my classroom processes.
- √   Refined my professional work plan and based it on the mission and goals of my department and school.
- √   Discussed my professional work plan with my dean.
- √   Constantly interviewed and surveyed my students as to the effectiveness of the teaching/learning system.
- √   Taught students additional TQI tools, including the use of portfolios for self-assessment.

Step 10: New activities constantly evolve from the old.
- √   Presented the competencies that the students are expected to achieve during the semester.
- √   Reaffirmed that all classroom processes are student-focused.
- √   Constantly revised my vision of the optimal learning environment.
- √   Co-created learning experiences with the students.
- √   Integrated many of the learning experiences and demonstrated how they relate to the real world.
- √   Facilitated new activities that arose from the old.

Chapter 11:   There must be an audience beyond the professor.

In the past, educators have created assignments that students "do for them." That is to say, the professor creates the assignments based on the scope and sequence of the course in the curriculum, and students complete the assignments and turn them in to the professor who grades and returns them to the student. The cycle goes from professor to student to professor to student.

Professor

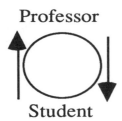

Student

In this model, the student performs work for the professor and solely for the professor. Seldom is there any intrinsic reward or pride in workmanship. It is an illusion to imagine that students complete their work in traditional classrooms for anyone but the professor, although occasionally, a student will be motivated by wanting to please parents or some other adult figure. Some students do learn and complete complex tasks because they see the inherent virtue in doing it or because they know this is but one step along a long road towards some far-off career goal. It is a wonder that so many students complete their work, especially when considering how irrelevant so many assignments are.

In the above model, the professor is the final customer. In other words, the professor has to be "satisfied" if the student is to be rewarded with a grade. The classroom becomes "professor-centered," rather than "student-centered."

Perhaps we would be better off thinking about course competencies rather than assignments. In quality classrooms, students are responsible for co-creating the learning experiences required to demonstrate the mastery of competencies. By engaging in this exercise, students create experiences that have meaning to them.

What motivates human behavior is not producing for others, but producing or creating something for ourselves. When students have break-through learning, they experience an exhilaration that extends far beyond the satisfaction of performing a task because they have been told to do so.

Pride in workmanship comes from performing feats and solving "puzzles" that are a stretch beyond our current limitations. It comes from the good feelings about being able to do something for oneself.

Humans are naturally curious, and in courses where experiences for exploration are encouraged, the students become better problem solvers and engage in higher-level thinking skills. In courses where rote memorization and learning by regurgitating facts is a way of life, less critical thinking, less creativity, and less curiosity are achieved. These students may have learned to memorize and remember long enough to give back answers on a test, but they've learned nothing about how to collect many sources of information to generate a hypothesis or create new knowledge from previously learned material. In the latter case, students "learn" because someone directs them. In the former case, natural curiosity and invention make learning a joy, and the resulting product is a source of great pride to the student, her/his parents, peers, and others.

As an example, consider this scenario with some professors who wanted to establish a "Learning Community" for at-risk students who were entering as freshmen. The previous spring the professors got together and agreed that they would work together with students to eliminate all busywork and combine assignments in World Geography, English Composition, and Economics. The three professors agreed that they would team teach each class from 9:00 AM to noon on Monday, Wednesday, and Friday. The 60 students would receive 9 semester hours of credit. They would be advised by these professors, and would receive special help on Tuesdays and Thursdays, as requested. The professors agreed to show the inter-relationships between the world economy and world geography. The essay exams would be corrected for the English Composition portion of the credit. Students and teachers together could co-create the experiences. Since this was new for the professors (also for the students), they were somewhat concerned about how this would happen, but were determined to forge ahead. Since students and professors were already organized into teams (with administrative approval), it provided an organizational pattern that could work.

In the fall, professors gathered and asked the students for suggestions about what interested them and explained that the plan was to build educational experiences around their interests. With some guidance the students were able to list a wide range of topics. Next, the professors led the group in a discussion of "how do you want to learn about these things." This naturally led to "what will the product of our education be...or how will we demonstrate that we've learned."

The sixty students were placed into ten teams ranging in size from 3 to 10. Each team conducted research on a variety of topics such as the role of trade routes and regional religions, beliefs, and economy. No less that 58 of the students completed the competencies of the Learning Community with grades of A's or B's. The students and professors became very excited about the possibilities of performing this type of experiment with other courses.

In the Spring, the students went on to other classes—the traditional type. Unfortunately approximately 40 of the students have dropped out of college.

Other Learning Community possibilities between courses in English, Speech, Art, History, Sociology, Science, Computer Science, and Mathematics are possible. Professors can work together and provide common learning experiences that allow students to prepare one or more significant pieces of research that can be assessed by professors of each discipline for style and content.

STUDENTS' HOPES AND DREAMS

At all levels of education, you should invite others into your course regularly. Allow students to share with their peers what they are working on. They should be able to explain how any learning experience relates to the required competencies, and if they are going to go beyond the required competencies to attain much higher levels of learning, that, too, should be noted. Empower students to speak to a variety of people since they assume a lead role in the learning experience. This expands students' abilities to communicate with older adults as well as enables them to demonstrate pride in workmanship. The focus of any course must remain on the students, since they are the reason for colleges.

Portfolios also provide a means of demonstrating growth in knowledge and capabilities. Students determine what belongs in their portfolios based on the **Quality Factors** agreed upon by the class and their own sense of "best" work. Since students are selecting their best work for the portfolio, it follows that they are in the best position to relate this information to parents, peers, and other people.

Other ways to demonstrate student growth is by producing videos of them in action. Students truly enjoy seeing the results of their progress. A videotape also provides valuable feedback to the student(s). Teams of students can critique their own teamwork and their results. Individual students can do a self-assessment of their progress and be taught to look for the quality factors. Teams and individuals can even be taught to critique each other's work and thereby provide valuable feedback. In the end, the results of any videotaped experience can extend far beyond the particular learning experience that has just been completed.

VOLUNTEER OR SERVICE LEARNING

While it is important for students to experience pride in creating educational products that extend beyond the classroom, it is also important for students to give back to their community and thus gain a sense of oneness with their community. Some colleges have implemented a volunteer project as a requirement for graduation. I believe that service work or volunteerism can and probably should become a part of everyone's educational experiences each academic year (beginning in kindergarten).

The experiences that students co-create can easily include volunteerism. Also, intergenerational volunteer experiences can help provide a connection to other adults that is often missing in the lives of many youth.

ΔΔΔΔΔΔΔΔ

The following is a checksheet tool to help the professor to implement the **Quality Fusion** technique into the classroom.

Step 1:   The mission, goals, and academic integrity of your course are absolutely clear.
   √   Established a course mission statement.
   √   Developed personal goals for the course.
   √   Communicated mission and goals to the students.
   √   Aligned course mission and goals with those of the department (program/major).

Step 2:   You are demonstrating leadership.
   √   Developed a definition of a total quality classroom.
   √   Walk-the-Talk about quality.
   √   Understand Deming's system of **Profound Knowledge**.
   √   Use a variety of teaching styles.
   √   Have a CQI program for self and for students.

Step 3:   All work is pertinent and flows from the students.
   √   Broke down barriers on day one by establishing a course mission statement with the students.
   √   Had students co-create learning experiences.
   √   Stressed the importance of teamwork in problem solving and decision making.
   √   Defined quality and what it means.
   √   Created interdisciplinary learning activities.

Step 4:   The course content is connected to the surrounding community and the real world.
   √   Demonstrated the connectedness between work and the real world.
   √   Asked the students to analyze the learning assignments.
   √   Began TQM training for the students.
   √   Implemented student suggestions on how best to improve the learning system.

Step 5:   The student is treated as a "worker," but s/he is also considered a valuable team member of the "research and development" department.

√   Gave the students an historical overview about the quality movement and discussed examples.

√   Discussed the P-D-C-A cycle and root causes of problems.

Step 6:   Peer teaching, small group work, and team work are emphasized.

√   Engaged the students in activities that emphasized teaming and making learning fun.

√   Engaged students to work independently away from the team, but encouraged them to report the results to their peers.

√   Provided guidelines and opportunities for students to assess each others' work.

√   Emphasized the systems approach and regularly asked the students how we could reduce fear.

√   Provided students with the opportunity for peer tutoring.

√   Elaborated upon the types of quality teams.

√   Introduced the students to additional TQI tools and techniques.

Step 7:   Students should have aesthetic experiences.

√   Encouraged students to use their imagination daily.

√   Discussed the importance of art, music, nature, relaxation techniques, meditation, diet, and exercise with one or more of my students.

√   Discussed news headlines and/or controversial topics with one or more of the students.

√   Gathered specific data to evaluate and improve creative experiences.

Step 8:   Classroom processes include reflection.

√   Developed instant feedback form with students in order to measure classroom processes.

√   Distributed instant feedback forms in order to examine classroom processes.

√   Reflected on my mission, goals, and classroom processes.

√   Set time aside for students to reflect on the relevance of course work to real world issues and encouraged them to discuss their perceptions.

√   Developed self-assessment and goal-setting instruments with students.

Step 9:   The teaching/learning system is constantly evaluated.
√   Used modified Malcolm Baldrige Quality Award Criteria to judge the effectiveness of my classroom processes.
√   Refined my professional work plan and based it on the mission and goals of my department and school.
√   Discussed my professional work plan with my dean.
√   Constantly interviewed and surveyed my students as to the effectiveness of the teaching/learning system.
√   Taught students additional TQI tools, including the use of portfolios for self-assessment.

Step 10: New activities constantly evolve from the old.
√   Presented the competencies that the students are expected to achieve during the semester.
√   Reaffirmed that all classroom processes are student-focused.
√   Constantly revised my vision of the optimal learning environment.
√   Co-created learning experiences with the students.
√   Integrated many of the learning experiences and demonstrated how they relate to the real world.
√   Facilitated new activities that arose from the old.

Step 11: There is an audience beyond the Professor.
√   Encouraged students to "dream" about what they want to do in the future.
√   Allowed students to invite others into the classroom and to share with them what they are working on.
√   Encouraged students to share their portfolios with parents, other professors, and visitors.
√   Extended learning experiences into the community.

Summary

The benefits of using total quality management processes in the classroom are enormous. The synergy creates an experience that engages all students to become active-partners in their education. For generations, we (educators) have created a climate that encouraged students to become passive learners. With the examples in this book, I've attempted to demonstrate successful ways professors can impact the lives of their students by exciting them about learning, empowering them to become actively engaged in continuous improvement, and encouraging them to work in partnership with professor and fellow students to improve the classroom processes.

**Now The
Journey
Begins!**

The responsibility for improving the classroom and all its processes, rests with the professor. Leadership must precede action and improvement. I hope that I provided some guidelines upon which to act.

Prior to beginning, be certain that you have a thorough understanding of the theory of total quality improvement. This is a necessity; otherwise, you're apt to select those elements that most nearly complement your current paradigms and disregard those that seem in conflict. Study the theory through the eyes of the late W. Edwards Deming, J.M. Juran, Philip Crosby, and other quality experts. Include in your studies, works by Dr. William Glasser, particularly *The Quality School,* since he addresses the issue of student responsibility, albeit the K-12 classroom. A must reading is my previous book *The Quality Professor*—actually it should be read prior to this book since it gives the principles of TQM, the total quality improvement tools and techniques mentioned in this book, as well as a self-assessment tool based on the Malcolm Baldrige Quality Award Criteria.

Once you begin implementing quality improvement processes in the classroom it is necessary to continue learning and reading about quality. What may seem so simple at first, becomes rather complex when you try to implement it. Armed with a thorough understanding, you'll be in a better position to discuss continuous quality improvement with colleagues, administrators, parents, students and the general public.

If your college has not adapted the principles of quality, there will be an even more important need for you to be an articulate spokesperson for the new ways you'll be working within your classroom. Only by your own continuous improvement journey and study will you feel adequately prepared to meet whatever challenges may come your way. I cannot emphasize enough the need to start on a program of continuous education and improvement yourself.

My goal has been to draw connections for the reader to ways to meld continuous quality improvement into an educational system that succeeds in expanding the learning experiences for all students. I have spoken repeatedly of the concept of continuous improvement and hope that you've been able to grasp that every classroom process and every learning experience is a potential continuous improvement project.

I must follow them; I am their leader.

Andrew Bonar Law

Throughout your course, engage students in leadership roles for improvement. Have them collect data for system change and also for personal change. Combine debriefing exercises with regular customer satisfaction surveys. These will provide you with valuable information. Be certain to inform students and others of the feedback you're getting and encourage their participation by providing suggestions for improvement. Each of these activities will lend great value to your improvement efforts.

The time has come for educators to realize that things can and must be improved for the sake of students, communities, and the nation. No one can afford to rest on current levels of success—continuous improvement must become a way of life—every day and in every way. As educators, we have an obligation to be role models for this philosophy and mentor students to become problem solvers.

Great colleges and great classrooms share these elements:
- Trust
- Pride
- Quality
- Fun

Begin today to create the quality classroom that you imagined earlier in this book, and don't be distracted by those who say "it cannot be done." More and more professors across the nation are joining the move to continuous quality learning. They have ceased blaming students, parents, administration, government, or others for the problems that beset them and realize that it is the system that is keeping everyone (including themselves) from being successful.

My advice is to confront whatever fears you may have about empowering students and letting go of control and move forward in spite of them! Continue to push the limits of your comfort zone and you'll experience feelings of renewal that will encourage you to continue.

Remember, this approach is not a vaccine! It is not a quick fix! However, by following these suggestions, you will witness gradual improvements that can be sustained over time while making additional improvements. Don't be discouraged because you think improvement is coming too slowly, or if mistakes are made along the way. My experience is that students, provided there is a trusted and respectful environment, will want to help. The name of the Total Quality Game is continuous improvement. This means that problems are viewed as opportunities for improvement. Patience, persistence, and belief will carry the day.

Good luck! You can make a difference!

References

Barker, Joel. *Future Edge: Discovering the New Paradigms of Success.* New York, NY: Wm. Morrow & Co., Inc., 1992.

Byrnes, Margaret A., Cornesky, Robert A., and Byrnes, Lawrence W. *The Quality Teacher: Implementing Total Quality Management in the Classroom.* Port Orange, FL: Cornesky & Associates, Inc. 1992.

Byrnes, Margaret and Robert A. Cornesky. *Quality Fusion: Turning Total Quality Management Into Classroom Practice.* Port Orange, FL: Cornesky & Associates Press, 1994.

Cornesky, R.A., Ron Baker, Cathy Cavanaugh, William Etling, Michael Lukert, Sam McCool, Brian McKay, An-Sik Min, Charlotte Paul, Paul Thomas, David Wagner, and John Darling. *Using Deming to Improve Quality in Colleges and Universities,* Madison, WI: Magna Publications, Inc., 1989.

Cornesky, R.A., Sam McCool, Larry Byrnes, and Robert Weber. *Implementing Total Quality Management in Institutions of Higher Education.* Madison, WI: Magna Publications, Inc., 1991.

Cornesky, R.A. and Sam McCool. *Total Quality Improvement Guide for Institutions of Higher Education.* Madison, WI: Magna Publications, Inc., 1992.

Cornesky, R.A. *The Quality Professor: Implementing Total Quality Management in the College Classroom.* Madison, WI: Magna Publications, Inc., 1993.

Covey, Stephen R. *The 7 Habits of Highly Effective People.* New York, NY: Simon & Schuster, 1989.

Crosby, Philip B. *Quality Without Tears: The Art of Hassle-Free Management.* New York, NY: McGraw-Hill Book Co., 1984.

Deming, W. Edwards. *Out of the Crisis.* Cambridge, MA: Productivity Press or Washington, DC: The George Washington University, MIT-CAES, 1982.

Glasser, William. *The Quality School.* New York, NY: Harper & Row. 1990.

Glasser, William. *The Quality School Teacher*. New York, NY: Harper Collins Publishers, Inc. 1993.

Wigginton, Eliot. *Sometimes a Shining Moment: The Foxfire Experience*. New York, NY: Doubleday, 1985.